Anatomy of a Lynching

Anatomy of a Lynching

The Killing of Claude Neal

JAMES R. McGOVERN

Louisiana State University Press

Baton Rouge

Any man's death diminishes me, because I am involved in
Mankinde.

—John Donne
Devotions, XVII

Copyright © 1982 by Louisiana State University Press
All rights reserved
Manufactured in the United States of America

Designer: Albert Crochet
Typeface:Trump Medieval
Typesetter: Graphic Composition, Inc.
Printer and binder: Thomson-Shore, Inc.

The author wishes to thank the Alabama State
Archives, Montgomery, for permission to quote
"The Confession of Claude Neals" and the
Florida State Archives, Tallahassee, for
permission to quote the letter from M. B. Collie
to Governor David Sholtz, November 12, 1934.

LIBRARY OF CONGRESS CATALOGING IN PUBLICATION DATA

McGovern, James R.
  Anatomy of a lynching.

  Bibliography: p.
  Includes index.
  1. Neal, Claude, d. 1934.   2. Lynching.
I. Title.
HV6465.F6M35   364.1'34   81–17140
ISBN 0-8071-1766-8 (paper)   AACR2

Louisiana Paperback Edition, 1992
01   00   99   98   5   4   3

The paper in this book meets the guidelines for permanence and dura-
bility of the Committee on Production Guidelines for Book Longevity of
the Council on Library Resources. ⊗

Contents

Figures

Preface and Acknowledgments

The Scottsboro case has preempted the attention of liberals and scholars as the *cause célèbre* of racism and its attendant violence in the South in the 1930s. Few remember a second event, the lynching of Claude Neal, a black, in Greenwood, Florida, October 27, 1934. The murder of Neal, which NAACP spokesman Walter White condemned as "one of the most bestial crimes ever committed by a mob," did not upstage the Scottsboro episode. Yet this incident, which prompted A. A. Brill, America's foremost psychoanalyst, to write, "De Sade in all his glory could not have invented a more diabolical situation," resulted in national news stories on the plight of the victim, produced an outcry from liberal organizations, and drew criticism from persons close to President Roosevelt.[1]

Both Neal and the Scottsboro boys had allegedly violated the South's most sacred taboo: sex between a black male and a white female. In retaliation, those who determined justice, the Alabama juries and the Florida lynchers, imposed severe penalties to deter further transgressions.

Though discrimination against blacks characterized American life and was acceptable to most Americans at this time, Scotts-

1. Walter White to William Rosenwald, November 16, 1934, A. A. Brill to Walter White, November 24, 1934, both in National Association for the Advancement of Colored People (NAACP) Papers, Manuscript Division, Library of Congress.

boro and the Neal lynching produced denunciations of racial injustice. This message was carried principally by the national media and also by the threat of action by the federal government.
Violence toward blacks, whether in a formal court of law in Alabama or under an oak tree in Jackson County, Florida, was increasingly unacceptable to the nation. The Scottsboro and Neal
cases hastened the emergence of a society which more nearly
practiced equality under the law for all its citizens.

The book that follows is concerned with more than the violent
death of Neal in the dark woods of northwest Florida. That story
should be recounted because of its drama and because the incident and its aftermath are indices of racial attitudes in America
at the time. But the presentation is concerned, too, with a larger
issue. It seeks to explain, with the Neal incident as a case study,
why the lynching of blacks persisted as a manifestation of American violence until the mid-1930s. New perspectives on this issue
are possible through examination of the Neal lynching and its
consequences, recent findings on racial aggression, and the decline and demise of lynching following the murder of Neal.

Definitions of lynching vary. The sense of federal legislation to
outlaw the practice in the 1930s sees lynching as an act of a mob,
usually three or more persons, which punishes and kills its victim wholly without authority of the law. This definition was
broadened by a special study group at Tuskegee Institute in 1940
to include motives for the mob, *i.e.*, "acting under the pretext of
service to justice, race or tradition." The meaning of lynching as
it is used in this book is less legalistic and conveys a more popular connotation, but one which clearly distinguishes it from murder. The key to the phenomenon is community approval, either
explicit, in the form of general participation by the local citizenry, or implicit, in the form of acquittal of the killers with or
without a trial. Approbation by the community is also usually
confirmed by such public activities of the lynch mob as a manhunt and chase and display of the victim's body in a conspicuous
place. From this perspective the practice of lynching virtually
disappears from the American scene after the 1930s. The reasons

for that disappearance reveal new insights on the nature of lynching itself.

Several people recall the 1934 incident. These include Neal's relatives and acquaintances and those of the white girl he was accused of raping and murdering, associates and friends of the lynch mob, and a few spectators. Only one of the lynchers is still living. No one interviewed wished to disclose his name. In fact information obtained about the lynching was conditional on his remaining anonymous. The author and his able research assistant, Walter T. Howard, obtained especially useful information from two persons, one the editor of a local newspaper at the time of the incident, and the other a close friend of the mob members to whom they related details of the lynching.

Jackson County, Florida, is still sensitive about the Neal lynching. Its violence has affected race relations in the area to this day. Of the ten blacks interviewed, several were initially reluctant to speak of the event. When they did furnish data they had first to be assured from recommendations by trustworthy persons that the author would not use the information to compromise them. Among this group, one, who obviously feared reprisals, remarked, "Well, if I am going down, it will be for a good cause." All had to be guaranteed anonymity.

Whites generally were more open, perhaps because of recommendations from friends on the staff of Chipola Junior College in Marianna, Florida. But with few exceptions, the interviews with fifteen whites inevitably reached a point of sensitivity indicating uneasiness among them as well.

There was an abundance of written materials to augment oral history on the Neal lynching. These included sheriff's reports, stories in local and national newspapers, findings of investigations by the governors of Florida and Alabama (the Florida lynch mob seized Neal from a south Alabama jail), and a sixteen-page report by an investigator who represented the NAACP on the scene within ten days of the lynching. The aftermath and effects of the lynching are also abundantly documented in the files of the NAACP, which contain more information on the Neal case than any other lynching in American history, and those of Florida's governor, David Sholtz, as well as in the correspondence of Eleanor and Franklin Roosevelt.

The author wishes to acknowledge the excellent aid he received from librarians and researchers at the Library of Congress both in its manuscript and photography divisions, the Franklin D. Roosevelt Library at Hyde Park, New York, the Florida State Archives at Tallahassee, the Florida History Library at the University of Florida, Gainesville, the Tuskegee Institute Archives at Tuskegee, Alabama, and the Schomburg Research Library in New York. He also wishes to acknowledge the important contribution of Mr. Odell Griffith, of Pensacola, Florida, whose knowledge of northwest Florida and critical skills have been invaluable to this study. Professor Jerome F. Coling, who contributed maps, and the reference staff at the University of West Florida Library also deserve the author's commendation.

Anatomy of a Lynching

Chapter 1

Lynch Law

In the early hours of October 27, 1934, in the deep woods of northwest Florida, a mob lynched a black laborer, Claude Neal. He was accused of raping and murdering an attractive young white woman, the daughter of one of his employers, just nine days earlier.

Neal was quickly jailed after the body of the young woman was discovered and some evidence began to implicate him. To forestall mob violence law officers removed Neal to jails in nearby counties and finally to Alabama. But after the mob located him, he was apprehended and returned to the site of his alleged crime. Despite an earlier protest by a local newspaper editor that one murder in Jackson County was enough, persons controlling Neal reacted with whiplike anger. He had seemingly forfeited his right to life by his bestial behavior and so they subjected him to great cruelty and finally lynched him. The events surrounding his death resembled a carnival. But the evidence against him was not totally convincing. Blacks whispered that a white man was responsible and that Neal's confession had been wrung from him under duress.

On the surface Neal's case was just another incident of a black being lynched in the South. He was one of nearly three thousand who had met a similar fate since the 1880s. But as events proved, the gruesome circumstances of his death contributed to a national abhorrence of the gala lynching celebration. The public's reaction probably contributed substantially to the end of that practice in the United States.

The American practice of lynching blacks, while sometimes employed in the antebellum South, became a systematic feature of race relations after 1865.[1] The worst period for lynching occurred after Reconstruction until 1900 when southern whites felt the need to reassert their authority over blacks.[2] Blacks had to be taught their place once again, especially to be dutiful and obedient to white employers and to suppress sexual impulses toward white women. Appropriately, the literature of this period in the South increasingly depicted blacks as bestial persons but also implied, paradoxically, that they could be restrained from their animal lusts and depravities by sadistic tortures and lynchings.[3]

Once southern whites felt themselves in comfortable command after 1900, lynchings gradually declined. The hangman's noose was still used to intimidate blacks, but especially after 1920 the phenomenon was very largely confined to the rural South.[4]

The average number of blacks reported lynched in the United States was per year 67 in the 1880s, 111 in the 1890s, 57 in the

1. Arthur F. Raper, *The Tragedy of Lynching* (Chapel Hill: University of North Carolina Press, 1933), 481; Allen W. Trelease, *White Terror: The Ku Klux Klan Conspiracy and Southern Reconstruction* (New York: Greenwood, 1972).

2. National Association for the Advancement of Colored People, *Thirty Years of Lynching in the United States, 1889–1918* (New York: National Association for the Advancement of Colored People, 1919), 31–32. Annual rates for lynchings are available in Monroe Work, *Negro Year Book* (Tuskegee, Alabama: Department of Records and Research, Tuskegee Institute) for nearly every year from 1912 to 1956. The earliest statistics on lynchings were gathered by the Chicago *Tribune* from 1882 to 1903. Cumulative data through 1968 can be found in Daniel T. Williams (comp.), *Eight Negro Bibliographies* (New York: Kraus Reprint Co., 1970), 6–15. All data on lynching is approximate because it represents reported lynchings only. There are no statistics available for lynchings in the antebellum periods.

3. George Frederickson, *The Black Image in the White Mind: The Debate On Afro-American Character and Destiny, 1871–1914* (New York: Harper and Row, 1971), especially 235–81. See also I. A. Newby, *Jim Crow's Defense: Anti-Negro Thought in America 1900–1930* (Baton Rouge: Louisiana State University Press, 1965).

4. Raper, *Tragedy of Lynching,* 28–29.

1910s, 28 in the 1920s, and 15 from 1930 to 1935. Almost all these lynchings took place in the South.

Despite the critical role lynching has occupied in the history of race relations in the South, there are no adequate historical analyses of the problem. Arthur Raper's *The Tragedy of Lynching*, a sociological treatment published in 1933, is still the classic interpretation.[5] The reason for this lack is that the essential data for objective analysis go unreported. Source materials on lynchings are scarce because there were no jury records. And since lynchings are murders, legitimated through community approval, even those who disapproved the practice would withhold information for fear of ostracism or personal safety. The local law enforcement system, meanwhile, would render innocuous and vapid accounts to local and state officials while outside investigators were seldom treated cooperatively. Therefore, it is doubtful if a team of scholars working with scraps of information from innumerable small towns could piece together a creditable history of the phenomenon.

The absence of carefully documented histories has not deterred an elaborate corpus of excellent sociological and psychological theory on the subject. Raper's study, based on quantitative data, establishes that lynchings after 1900 were more likely to occur in impoverished southern counties, especially in recently settled areas where blacks constituted less than one fourth of the population. Conditions there resembled the end of Reconstruction since tenuous social relations in those newer areas sometimes benefited blacks who were tempted to transgress customary caste lines. Small-town and backwoods southern whites living in such places often adhered to frontier ethics and were prone to admin-

5. Raper attempted to construct a "social anatomy" of lynchings which occurred in America in 1930. His interpretation, without documentation or evidence of the use of government records, is basically confined to socioeconomic analysis typical of the 1930s. Another useful work by an acute observer, who investigated over forty lynchings, is Walter White, *Rope and Faggot: A Biography of Judge Lynch* (New York: Knopf, 1929). The best interpretive analysis of lynching is Jacquelyn Dowd Hall, *Revolt Against Chivalry: Jessie Daniel Ames and the Woman's Campaign Against Lynching* (New York: Columbia University Press, 1979), 129–57.

ister justice vigilante style, face to face, rather than submit to cumbrous legal procedures. The poverty of the rural South, including many areas long populated, contributed as well to understaffed and inadequate law enforcement. Deficient communications and poor roads in these areas accentuated the problems. As a result, persons living along lonely rural roads were natural vigilantes. They were especially prone to the use of violence against blacks at times of depression in the cotton market.[6]

Not only persons from the poorer areas, but the poorer people in those areas were most likely to be conspicuous in lynch mobs.[7] They were themselves victims of the crop-lien system which developed in the South after the Civil War. Their poverty and indebtedness were linked to the one-crop, cotton system and exploitation by local furnishing men. The legacy of generations of poverty for poor white tenants and sharecroppers was crowded, wretched houses, limited motivation for improvement, hookworm and pellagra-ridden bodies, and year after year the same kinds of faded overalls, tired backs, and uneducated minds come sundown. Persons so bereft of real strengths gladly settled for what they could get. They may have been called by various names, "crackers," "rednecks," "hillbillies," "po' white trash," and "po' buckra," but at least they were whites. For such persons, lynching might become a major solace and hence a substitute for the amenities of life common to larger and more prosperous communities.[8] It seems hardly coincidental that the peak periods for

6. Richard Maxwell Brown notes the connection between vigilantism and poor transportation and communications in rural areas in "Vigilantism in America" in H. Jon Rosenbaum and Peter C. Sederberg (eds.), *Vigilante Politics* (Philadelphia: University of Pennsylvania Press, 1976), 80–109, especially 92–93. See also Raper, *Tragedy of Lynching*, 18, 28–29. On the relation between lynchings and a downswing in cotton prices, see T. J. Woofter in Raper, *Tragedy of Lynching*, 31, and Alexander Mintz, "A Re-Examination of Correlations between Lynchings and Economic Indices," in Allen D. Grimshaw (ed.), *Racial Violence in the United States* (Chicago: Aldine Press, 1969), 349–53.

7. Raper, *Tragedy of Lynching*, 11.

8. There are numerous outstanding studies of poor whites in the South in the early decades of the twentieth century. Among the best are James Agee and Walker Evans, *Let Us Now Praise Famous Men* (Boston: Houghton Mifflin, 1941), Arthur D. Raper, *Tenants of the Almighty* (Chapel Hill: University of North Carolina Press, 1943), and Rupert B. Vance, *Human Factors in Cotton Culture: A Study in*

lynching coincided with a paltry per capita income gain in the South of less than 1 percent per year. Between 1900 and the Great Depression the number of lynchings declined when economic conditions improved, returns from cotton production per acre rising from $16.76 in 1902 to $35.14 in 1922.[9]

Several classic sociological studies on race relations in the South in the 1930s and early 1940s confirm Raper's view that the lynching of blacks was confined largely to the poor rural South. They delineate additional motives for lynching by focusing on the caste gains which the practice conferred on whites. John Dollard observed that lynchings seldom met disapproval from local townsfolk regardless of class or education. This is because all whites benefited from their upper-caste solidarity and lynching was one of the most effective instruments to assure their dominance. Whites thereby enjoyed cheap labor from black sharecroppers and workers, sexual favors from black women, and deference and prevention of miscegenation between black males and white females (a gender as well as a caste gain). Local police therefore could not risk massive community displeasure by resisting lynch mobs, and ministers had first to think that their opposition might alienate prominent members of their congregations.[10] Indeed, any white who balked at the caste system and attempted to initiate personal as against caste relationships with blacks ran the risk of severe social ostracism, especially in the small towns and rural areas.

Since the preservation of caste advantages for whites ultimately depended on their acknowledgment by blacks, a critical intent of lynching was to intimidate assertive blacks. Lynching produced the requisite terror. Bands of men roaming at night, striking at will, dragging blacks out of cabins or jails and leaving

---

the Social Geography of the American South (Chapel Hill: University of North Carolina Press, 1929).

9. Roger L. Ransom and Richard Sutch, *One Kind of Freedom: The Economic Consequences of Emancipation* (Cambridge: Cambridge University Press, 1977), 18; Vance, *Human Factors in Cotton Culture*, 125.

10. John Dollard, *Caste and Class in a Southern Town* (Garden City: Doubleday, 1957), especially 315–63. See also Raper, *Tragedy of Lynching*, 13, 20–23.

their ghastly remains as a public spectacle best assured white dominance. Lynch violence was made more frightening because whites seemingly administered it capriciously.[11] An angry mob might be incited on a hot summer day to give public notice to all blacks by hanging one of them for merely walking or talking out of place or failing to show proper deference or disobeying an order.

Most blacks responded by fearfully staying within prescribed social boundaries. It is doubtful if any black male growing up in the rural South in the period 1900 to 1940 was not traumatized by a fear of being lynched. Dollard noted that in "Southerntown," "the threat of lynching is likely to be in the mind of the Negro child from earliest days. Memories of such events came out frequently in the life history of Negroes."[12] Somewhere, sometime, like overalls, the advent of body hair, or the death of a loved one, came another fact of life to a black male— the sickening fear that he might be accused of something and suddenly find himself in a circle of tormentors with no one to help him.

Caste sanctions proved an arbitrary mechanism for maintaining interracial equilibrium because blacks perceived the system's injustice and because whites feared or imagined blacks were restive. This became the pressure point for "a bursting of the steam boiler of the white man's frustration over 'keeping the Negro in his place.' "[13] Lynching then became *the* resolvent of "periodic trouble between the castes."

> Periodically there seems to develop a situation in which a number of Negroes begin to rebel against the caste restrictions. This is not an open revolt but a gradual pressure, in which, little by little, they move out of the strict pattern of approved behavior. The whites feel this pressure and begin to express resentment. They say the Negroes are

11. Dollard, *Caste and Class*, 216; Gunnar Myrdal, Richard Sterner, and Arnold Rose, *An American Dilemma: The Negro Problem and Modern Democracy* (New York: Harper and Row, 1944), 559.

12. Dollard, *Caste and Class*, 331. See also Charles S. Johnson, *Growing Up in the Black Belt: Negro Youth in the Rural South* (Washington: American Council on Education, 1941), 316–17; Richard Wright, *Black Boy: A Record of Childhood and Youth* (Reprint; New York: Harper and Row, 1966), 65.

13. Dollard, *Caste and Class*, 314.

getting "uppity," that they are getting out of their place and that something should be done about it. Frequently, the encroachment has been so gradual that the whites have no very definite occurrence to put their hands on; that is, most of the specific acts have been within the variations ordinarily permitted, yet close enough to the limits of variation to be irritating to the whites. Finally, the hostility of the whites reaches such a pitch that any small infraction will spur them to open action. A Negro does something which ordinarily might be passed over, or which usually provokes only a mild punishment, but the whites respond with violence. The Negro victim then becomes both a scapegoat and an object lesson for his group. He suffers for all the minor caste violations which have aroused the whites, and he becomes a warning against future violations. After such an outburst, the Negroes again abide strictly by the caste rules, the enmity of the whites is dispelled, and the tension relaxes. The whites always say after such an outburst: "We haven't had any trouble since then."[14]

The violation of the caste code most certain to provoke a lynching was for a black to rape or have sexual relations with a white woman, invariably construed as rape as well.[15] The black offender thereby struck at the ultimate taboo. Behind this violent act lay a fantastic, unacceptable claim: black males would have sex with upper-caste women. If this "equality" were conceded all claims would have to be honored and the system would collapse. Under the circumstances sentiment and ideology could be easily invoked to justify draconic reprisals, including lynching. The innocence and sexual purity of southern white women contrasting with the depraved animalism of the black rapist and the misfortune that women so accosted would later have to appear in court to confess their ignominy became self-evident truths.[16] While

14. Allison Davis, Burleigh B. Gardner, and Mary R. Gardner, *Deep South: A Social Anthropological Study of Caste and Class* (Chicago: University of Chicago Press, 1941), 48–49.

15. Dollard, *Caste and Class*, 164–65. See also Donald L. Grant, *The Anti-Lynching Movement: 1883–1932* (San Francisco: R and E Research Associates, 1975), 13.

16. Anne Firor Scott, *The Southern Lady: From Pedestal to Politics, 1830–1930* (Chicago: University of Chicago Press, 1970) and Winthrop Jordan, *White over Black: American Attitudes Toward the Negro, 1550–1812* (Chapel Hill: University of North Carolina Press, 1968), 137–84, describe social expectations for white women in the South. Literature on the subject of the black man's inordinate cravings for white women is vast. It is well covered in Newby, *Jim Crow's Defense*, 136–38, and Frederickson, *The Black Image in the White Mind*, 272–82.

whites may have attributed lustful sexuality to blacks partly as a projection for their own wishes or practices with black women, they proclaimed only chivalric motives. Nor was there any hint of sexual envy of black males or any implication that their role as protectors also guaranteed their authority over the women protected.[17] Although white males in the South saw themselves as shouldering a heavy burden in upholding civilized values on behalf of their women, they were probably unaware of the extent to which they created that burden for themselves. Because of their insistence on the white woman's sexual naïveté and the black man's inordinate sexual cravings for her, white southern males condemned themselves to obsessive vigilance and to exaggerated actions against blacks who allegedly violated the social code. While there were in reality many virtuous southern women and a small and disturbing number of black male rapists, the energy expended by white males on the rape question was disproportionate to the problem. The chance of a white woman in the South being raped by a black male was probably not much greater than that of her being struck dead by lightning.

Southern white males persevered with their rape mythology because it was functional; caste and gender gains outweighed the price of continuous vigilance. Besides, it provided a story which simplified the problems of day-to-day living in a poor, biracial society.[18]

Recent interpretations of lynching have stressed psychological rather than caste or sociological considerations. They stress that the most prejudicial and violent persons are frequently "solid citizen types," people who, on the surface at least, are making a go of it in life, not the desperate malcontents or acknowledged monstrous perverts who wish to destroy because they are total

17. Several scholars have stated or implied that sexual fears of black males by white males account for their extreme aggression against blacks. See Dollard, *Caste and Class*, 160–61, 325, for comments on preoccupation of whites with supposed large-sized genitals of black males. For a description of similar fears in the colonial period see Jordan, *White over Black*, 79–83, 137–54. On lynchings as an aspect of gender domination, see Hall, *Revolt Against Chivalry*, 148–57.

18. Hall, *Revolt Against Chivalry*, 149.

outsiders. According to these interpretations, violence is often perpetrated by "conventional people" living in conformist societies. These persons compensate for feelings of inadequacy by violent attacks on scapegoats or the relatively defenseless while carefully identifying with the established sociopolitical order.[19] Arendt argues that Eichmann and his type of "organization man" were more interested in establishing their usefulness to the Nazi authorities than venting hostility toward the Jews. The fact that they also did the latter suggests how easily aggression can be displaced on weak people to incur social advantage. These types could easily divert anger from inviolate agents of authority, their parents, traditions, and the local power structure to groups such as blacks. They would readily stereotype blacks in negative terms and, with sufficient provocation, could easily form a lynch mob. They might even congratulate themselves for being men enough to assume the big responsibilities required by the community, without suspecting that their only daring was to give chase, not to do battle. Since southern society typically prized traditions and conformity, especially in rural areas, it would seem an ideal refuge for the authoritarian personality.

Erich Fromm, in a somewhat similar vein, has emphasized the joylessness of societies which exploit groups in their midst since they coerce conformity and thwart normal expression and hence generate destructiveness. Persons so governed by taboos and traditions resemble zombies, and their societies, psychically speaking, valleys of the dead. Lynchings, or the tearing apart of bodies, reliably reveal their morbid personalities and preoccupations and, at the same time, provide lurid sensationalism which contributes to their illusion of being alive.

The most productive line in recent theory about lynching, which enriches earlier explanations, is derived from empirical psychology. It asserts that violence toward blacks was most likely to occur when inhibitory influences were too weak to offset in-

---

19. T. W. Adorno, *et al.*, *The Authoritarian Personality* (New York: Harper, 1950), especially pages 384–89; Hannah Arendt, *Eichmann in Jerusalem: A Report on the Banality of Evil* (New York: Viking, 1948); Rosenbaum and Sederberg (eds.), *Vigilante Politics*, especially 3–29.

stigations.[20] Accordingly, whites attacked blacks primarily because they exercised virtually unlimited power over them. Since they did not anticipate effective retaliation from blacks or from civil authority they were emboldened to vent their anger without restraint.

If lynch mobs were to experience censure or punishment, these would have come in order of immediacy from (1) opposition of local whites who disapproved before the mob made its plans or at least before it began to abuse its victim; (2) effective local law enforcement to assure swift and nondiscriminatory action against the mob for inciting riots and other criminal deeds; (3) hostility and possible retaliation by blacks; (4) the state's enforcement of strict laws to assure cooperation by local and county officials; and (5) disapproval by public opinion nationally, reflected in educational and news media, and in statements from the churches and political leaders.

Opposition from fellow townsmen was rare in the rural South. To oppose a lynching would be to forfeit one's position in the white community because this type of action would jeopardize advantages of caste solidarity in which all whites shared. Although the identities of lynchers were generally known and they were even at times photographed, there were few outcries against them.[21] Nor were leaders of the mob always poor riffraff. One sheriff conceded that he had to give up his intentions to defend a black about to be lynched because "the first half-a-dozen men standing there were leading citizens—businessmen, leaders of their church and the community—I just couldn't do it."[22]

Lynchers were basically confident they could take their vic-

20. Erich Fromm, *The Anatomy of Human Destructiveness* (New York: Holt, Rinehart and Winston, 1973), 288–99; Leonard Berkowitz, *Aggression: A Social Psychological Analysis* (New York: McGraw-Hill, 1962), 46. Berkowitz also refers to lynching on pages 45, 58, 59, 80, 85, 115, 136–37. See also Albert Bandura, "Influence of Models' Reinforcement Contingencies on the Acquisition of Imitative Responses," *Journal of Personality and Social Psychology*, I (1965), 589–95.

21. Raper, *Tragedy of Lynching*, 20–24. The Collection of the Association of Southern Women for the Prevention of Lynching (Trevor-Arnett Library, Atlanta University) contains numerous photographs of lynch mobs.

22. Hall, *Revolt Against Chivalry*, 140.

tims without incrimination. Nearly half of the persons lynched in the 1920s (44.1 percent) never came under the custody of the law. During 1925 and 1926, for example, when the NAACP records fifty-two lynchings, there were, according to Monroe H. Work of Tuskegee Institute, only seven which brought indictments and convictions. Work's research established that there were seventy-five persons indicted in these seven lynchings of whom thirty were later convicted. Of these, five were given suspended sentences, one thirty days in jail, and fifteen prison terms from six to eight years. Overall, between 1900 and 1930 it is estimated that only 0.8 percent of lynchings in the United States were followed by criminal conviction of the lyncher.[23]

Lynch mobs would probably have been less inclined to aggress against blacks capable of retaliation.[24] Practically speaking, however, that capacity was severely undermined in the early decades of the twentieth century by considerations of survival among blacks as well as their pervasive fatalism and sense of inferiority.

If blacks had reacted angrily after lynchings results would probably also have been different. Instead, they generally became despondent and tried even more to placate the dominant caste. This tactic may have strengthened the resolve of whites to continue the practice. It is interesting to compare the effects of this resigned attitude among southern blacks with black experience in the North. There, blacks fought back in the race riots following World War I. Whereas the police at first had sided with the rioters against blacks, once the latter began to defend themselves and

23. Raper, *Tragedy of Lynching*, 31–32; White, *Rope and Faggot*, 224–25; James H. Chadbourn, *Lynching and the Law* (Chapel Hill: University of North Carolina Press, 1933), 13–14.

24. M. and E. Donnerstein, "Variables in Interracial Aggression: Potential Ingroup Censure," *Journal of Personality and Social Psychology*, XXVII (1975), 143–50. Using "aggression machines" or push-button switches to deliver aggression to "black targets" for errors on learning tasks, one half of the students were told their responses (*i.e.*, aggressions) would be made public and hence available to a liberal student group, and one half were led to believe that their answers would be kept private. The testing established that the students who knew their responses would be monitored and, in this situation, probably reproved, delivered a lower level of aggression to "black targets" than the group which felt free to deliver its feelings without fear of being censured.

communities became enmeshed in urban wars, police became more neutral in racial disputes, and the number and scope of explosive riots quickly subsided.[25]

State officials did not take effective action against lynchers either. State control over law enforcement agencies in local communities and counties, with noteworthy exceptions, was either lax or nonexistent. In the state of Florida, for example, where the largest number of blacks were lynched relative to the size of its black population of any state in the country, there was not a single conviction for lynching between 1900 and 1934, when Claude Neal was executed. Indeed, Florida's fundamentalist governor, Sidney J. Catts (1916–1920), actually declared he would himself resort to vigilante justice. Replying to an official of the NAACP who criticized the number of unpunished lynchings in Florida, Governor Catts retorted, "If any man, White or Black should dishonor one of my family he would meet my pistol square from the shoulder and every white man in the South, who is a red-blooded American, feels the same as I do."

Only six states in the 1930s had disciplinary statutes prohibiting lynchings, four of them in the South—Alabama, Kentucky, North Carolina, and South Carolina. A small number of states also imposed fines against cities or counties where lynchings took place, and others provided for the ouster of sheriffs who failed to prevent mob action.[26]

It is obvious, however, from the small number of convictions against lynchers that most of these laws were ineffective because they lacked support of the citizenry and vigorous prosecution by state officials. Meanwhile, legislators generally resisted pleas by governors for permission to empower state's attorneys to conduct their own prosecutions against lynchers, to call out troops independent of the wishes of local officials, or to issue injunctions

25. Davis, Gardner, and Gardner, *Deep South,* 48–49; Arthur I. Waskow, *From Race Riot to Sit-In, 1919 to the 1960s: A Study in the Connection Between Conflict and Violence* (Garden City: Anchor, 1967), 209–18.

26. Chadbourn, *Lynching and the Law,* 13, 29–32, 48, 58; Sidney J. Catts to John R. Shillady, March 18, 1919 (copy), in Lynching File, Schomburg Library, New York, N.Y.

against lynch mobs. This neglect by state officials was critical in view of the federal government's policy of complete laissez-faire.

The most constructive efforts to effect changes in attitudes toward lynching in the 1920s and 1930s came through voluntary groups which promoted consciousness-raising against the abuse. There were three of these organizations: the NAACP, the Commission on Interracial Cooperation, and the Association of Southern Women for the Prevention of Lynching. Although differing in composition (the latter two were comprised almost exclusively of southern whites), and in objectives (the NAACP sought a federal antilynching bill while the Interracial Commission retained until 1935 faith in state action), each viewed lynching as the most objectionable feature of race relations in America.

The NAACP adopted the antilynching cause as its major interest in the 1920s and 1930s. Its leadership exploited the emotional impact of lynchings as a dramatic departure from the nation's ideals of equal opportunity. The NAACP's prime strategy was to publicize findings of its investigations in newspapers and to circulate this information among liberal organizations, thereby sensitizing public opinion to the need for passage of federal antilynching legislation such as the Dyer Bill (1922) or the Wagner-Costigan Bill (1934). After the NAACP intensified its campaign for a federal antilynching law, spurred by the death of Claude Neal, the number of lynchings throughout the country began to drop sharply. Undoubtedly, as the NAACP's Walter White himself declared, fear of federal controls frightened and inhibited those who otherwise would have joined lynch mobs.[27]

The Commission on Interracial Cooperation and the Association of Southern Women for the Prevention of Lynching comprised the first organized bodies of effective southern opposition to lynching.[28] Both had an important, if incalculable, impact on

27. Robert L. Zangrando, "The Efforts of the National Association for the Advancement of Colored People to Secure Passage of a Federal Anti-Lynching Law" (Ph.D. dissertation, University of Pennsylvania, 1963), 79–115, 440–43; Walter White, *A Man Called White: The Autobiography of Walter White* (New York: Viking, 1948), 42.
28. On the Commission on Interracial Cooperation and the Association of

opinion, especially among literate, urban, middle-class, white persons. The CIC began functioning in 1919 in response to the racial unrest following World War I and developed effective local organizations primarily in the major cities of the South. Leaders of the commission emphasized study of the problem of lynching and publication of its findings ("the quest for a preventive can only be undertaken after we have an understanding of what is to be prevented"). Its activities led to Arthur Raper's *The Tragedy of Lynching*, published in 1933, "copies of which were sent to every editor, public library and college library in the South." As a relatively conservative organization, opposed to federal antilynching legislation and to any basic upheaval in the caste system, the Interracial Commission helped broaden the base of opposition to lynching in the South. But most southerners in the 1920s were probably more sympathetic to the Klan than the commission. As Benjamin Mays observed, commission members had to "sneak and hide" even when they held meetings in their own churches.[29]

The Association of Southern Women for the Prevention of Lynching, an offshoot of the Interracial Commission, was vigorously led by Jessie Daniel Ames. Its tactics were similar to the commission but it quickly became an organization with a large membership. Founded in 1930, it already had 35,000 members in 1935. The ASWPL shocked many southerners because its women took such a forceful stand against a practice purportedly designed for their protection. Many of these ladies tried to educate their membership to the evils of lynching or to intercept lynching parties with telephone calls to governors and letters to editors. Their opposition to lynching undoubtedly created confusion among its adherents. It is probably for good reason that Benjamin Mays, president of Morehouse College, believed the ASWPL, rather

Southern Women for the Prevention of Lynching see Edward F. Burrows, "The Commission on Interracial Cooperation" (Ph.D. dissertation, University of Wisconsin, 1954). The source materials for these organizations are in the Trevor-Arnett Library, Atlanta University. See also Hall, *Revolt Against Chivalry*, for the ASWPL.

29. Wilma Dykeman and James Stokely, *Seeds of Southern Change: The Life of Will Alexander* (Chicago: University of Chicago Press, 1962), 138, 140; Benjamin F. Mays, *Born to Rebel: An Autobiography* (New York: Scribner's, 1971), 72.

than the churches, provided the strongest voice against lynchings in the South.[30]

Since it is unlikely that historians will ever be able to analyze the phenomenon of lynching comprehensively because of a dearth of valid empirical data, they will have to rely on theories and on those case studies where information is unusually abundant. Theorists have long been convinced that lynching is multicausal, triggered by provincialism, poverty, caste gains and solidarity, and role preservation. The most rewarding recent insights suggest that lynchings occurred because the rewards obtained (silencing fears, doing one's duty, protecting women, retaining caste dominance, releasing aggressions, providing entertainment) outweighed deterrents (fears of effective retaliation).

The following is a case study of one of America's last "classic lynchings," an incident which included every element of violence associated with the practice from a public manhunt to the public display of the victim's body. It is hoped that a careful analysis of the death of Claude Neal will facilitate understanding, with the aid of social and psychological theory, of the phenomenon of lynching itself.

---

30. Association of Southern Women for the Prevention of Lynching, *Lynching Is Wholesale Murder* (n.p., n.d.), 17–19; Mays, *Born to Rebel*, 243.

Chapter 2

Jackson County

They ain't no different from nobody else. . . . They mouth is cut cross ways ain't it? Well, long as you don't see no man wid they mouth cut up and down, you know they all lie jus like de rest of us.

Zora Hurston, *Mules and Men*

Jackson County, Florida, where Claude Neal grew up and lived, was prone to the lynching of blacks. Between 1900 and his death in 1934, six other blacks were put to death there by lynching—John Sanders, Doc Peters, Edward Christian, Hattie Bowman, Galvin Baker, and another whose name is not on record.[1] This count was one of the largest for any Florida county at a time when Florida had the highest ratio of lynchings to its black population of any state in the nation.

The natural beauty of Jackson County contrasted sharply with the racial turbulence of its history. To this day, the county enjoys a green, primeval innocence. Nature is very active and profuse in this one-thousand-square-mile area, so much so that it appears to be barely subdued and looks as if it could come back and bury civilization in two or three undisturbed growing seasons.

The local treescape is thick and varied. Cedar along the numerous rivers and creeks darken the water so that the Spanish moss which shrouds trees on the riverbanks appears gothic in its reflection. While the abundant oaks are more open and people-serving, they dispute by their antiquity man's proprietary claims.

1. National Association for the Advancement of Colored People, *Thirty Years of Lynching in the United States 1889–1918* (New York: National Association for the Advancement of Colored People, 1919), 53–56. See also "Lynching by Counties," in files of the Association of Southern Women for the Prevention of Lynching Papers, Trevor-Arnett Library, Atlanta University, Atlanta, Georgia.

Pines are densely massed in every direction as nature's first line of defense, and grey, spindly cypress with cottonmouth moccasins at their base abound in the great expanse of swampy lands throughout the county.

Farms standing in the 1930s were carved with difficulty from these dense woods and lowlands. The long lines of trees which served as property dividers or stood in clusters in the middle of farmland were signs of the weariness of generations with the struggle. Other clues were the farmhouses. They lacked the robust appearance of their counterparts in New England and the Midwest and were almost universally too small for the large families which inhabited them. They seldom had more than three or four rooms and fewer than seven or eight persons living in them when the parents were young or middle-aged.[2] As late as the 1930s, nearly all Jackson County farmers lived as their ancestors of the 1870s—in a land of kerosene lamps, screenless windows, hence dense swarms of houseflies and gnats in the summer, and wispy woodsmoke and cold in the winter. Many of them still used mules for transportation along the county's meandering, sandy roads.[3]

The heat of the sun, so essential to agricultural livelihood, also presented problems from June through September. There were spells during this period when only the strongest could work in the midday. Life for most would then come to a standstill, and the countryside became quiet for miles without end. At these times, the occasional jostling of young boys, barefoot, on their way to a creek might provide the only break in the silence.

The historical traditions of the people who lived in Jackson County made for uneasy race relations. The county abounded with cotton plantations and slaves during the antebellum period.

2. Nearly half of Jackson County's population of 31,000 was less than twenty-one years of age in 1930. *Sixteenth Census of the United States: 1940, Population, Vol. II, Characteristics of the Population, Pt. II*, 54. The author's numerous interviews with citizens of Jackson County who lived there in the 1930s provided descriptions of farmhouses and farm life.

3. There were three thousand cars registered in Jackson County in 1934, less than 1 percent of the cars registered in Florida. See Jerome Tyre, Chief of Registration Services, Division of Motor Vehicles, State of Florida, to author, December 14, 1977.

Cotton was taken on rivers by barges and slave power to an outlet on the Gulf. In the 1930s, white folks wrote nostalgically about those good days when "darkies" sang and cavorted on the riverbanks "full of frolic and play." This legacy from the antebellum period was reinforced by the effects of a minor Civil War battle fought in Marianna, on September 27 and 28, 1864, when 850 Union soldiers including the 82nd and 86th Negro Regiments defeated a force made up largely of local volunteers. That battle, which included the sacking of the community and the burning of Saint Luke's Episcopal Church ("one of the worst pieces of vandalism ever accomplished by Yankee Negro troops"), by the hated black hirelings of Yankees, was memorialized in the 1920s on the stone shaft in Confederate Park on Marianna's main street. It read in part, *where overwhelming Federal forces were stubbornly resisted by a home guard of old men and boys and a few sick and wounded Confederates at home on furlough. This company was known as the cradle and the grave." Unpleasant memories of that battle resurfaced as late as 1931 when a local newspaper editor asked citizens to reflect on that unhappy day when "our beautiful town was placed in the hands of an unmerciful enemy" and "most of our killed were butchered and beaten to death after they had surrendered by the infernal Negro troops who finding them in their power took advantage of it."[4] The better days of the Confederacy were not forgotten either. Confederate armies encamped in memory in Jackson County into the twentieth century. Surviving veterans supplied later generations with stories about their gallant comrades.

The Reconstruction period in Jackson County produced unusually angry feelings toward blacks and federal officials who legislated radical changes on their behalf.[5] Local whites may have felt the federal presence even more than in other parts of the state because an office of the Freedman's Bureau was established in Marianna. The bureau supervised contracts between blacks and

4. Marianna *Floridan*, June 26, 1931, p. 3.
5. The best book on Reconstruction in Florida is Jerrell H. Shofner, *Nor Is It Over Yet: Florida in the Era of Reconstruction, 1863–1877* (Gainesville: University of Florida Press, 1974).

their employers and rewarded blacks with rich lands, eighty acres at minimal cost, under the Homestead Act of 1866. Jackson County whites fiercely resisted the local government, which worked closely with the Freedman's Bureau, and it nearly collapsed in the face of lawlessness. Citizens determined to maintain white supremacy initiated a reign of terror which took more than 150 lives vigilante style in two years.[6] The situation became almost anarchical when during 1868–1870 the appointed sheriff was unable to serve warrants because public feeling was so inflamed against him. He actually feared for his life when he left the county seat and ran the risk of being beaten up on the streets even there.[7] Meanwhile, coroner's juries, grand juries, and petit juries refused to take steps to incriminate those who promoted disorder. On one occasion a crowd would not permit an inquest over the death of a black. White men also refused to serve on coroner's juries and intimidated blacks from doing so. Whites took justice into their own hands, however, and killed black thieves when it seemed that the Reconstruction government was lax toward them. They also made an example of blacks for lesser offenses. And those who abused blacks were not punished severely. Thus a Jackson County Negro woman was beaten by John Bates, struck by his son, and bitten by their dog. The instance was so flagrant that Bates and his son were tried in criminal court, but the punishment, five cents and costs, hardly served to deter others who would attack blacks.

By the 1880s local whites had been restored to power, and by 1890 most Negroes in Florida had ceased to vote and to exert influence on local government. As the leading authority on Reconstruction in Florida noted, the Jim Crow laws "re-inforced existing social customs [toward blacks] which had remained unchanged by post-Civil War developments."[8] The caste system served thereafter to stabilize race relations in Jackson County on terms favorable to whites.

6. *Ibid.*, 134.
7. William W. Davis, *The Civil War and Reconstruction in Florida* (Gainesville: University of Florida Press, 1964), 603.
8. Shofner, *Nor Is It Over Yet*, 130, 344.

Jackson County's population was almost entirely derived from the Southeast, principally Alabama and Georgia. Although there had been continuous settlement by Americans even before 1821, when Andrew Jackson received the area for the United States from Spain, most of Jackson County's population in the 1930s had lived there for only one or two generations. In 1890 there were merely 9,528 residents. Population grew rapidly thereafter, especially during the decade from 1905 to 1915 which saw an increase from 26,000 to 35,000 people, a gain of nearly 30 percent. Since most of the in-migrants were whites, there were dramatic changes in the percentages of blacks and whites in the county. As late as 1905, blacks comprised 55 percent of the population, but the surge of poor whites resulted in a 60 percent white population in 1930. The following table summarizes this changeover and the general growth of Jackson County.

	Black	White	Total Population
1905	14,246	12,564	26,824
1915	16,848	18,501	35,351
1925	14,097	18,672	33,122
1935	13,338	21,996	35,384

Nearly all the newcomers as well as the residual population were farmers or servicers of the farm population. Jackson County did not have an "urban territory" until Marianna's population reached 3,122 in 1925.[9]

Jackson County in the 1920s was mainly a collection of small- to medium-sized farms, supplied with essential needs by a diffusion of farm-servicing small towns, all of which were connected by sandy, clay roads to the county seat.[10] The small towns, Graceville, Cottondale, and Greenwood, whose populations barely exceeded a thousand, could hardly be distinguished from one an-

9. *Florida State Census*, 1915 (Tallahassee: n.p., 1915), 16 and Table 4; *Florida State Census*, 1925 (n.p., n.d.), 56; *Florida State Census*, 1935 (Winter Park, Florida: Orange Press, n.d.), 13, 91.

10. *Fifteenth Census of the United States: 1930, Agriculture, Vol. III, Type of Farm, Pt. II*, 490, indicates that more than two-thirds of the farms in Jackson County were worth less than one thousand dollars.

other. One might be noted as "the largest single shipping point in the world for watermelons" and for its having a cotton gin, and another as a center of the local peanut industry and for having a sawmill, but they all had the same unpaved streets, predictable Baptist and Methodist churches, gasoline stations and garages, small banks and high schools.[11]

The country store stood next to the churches in importance in these towns. Indeed, if the menfolk were allowed to be fully honest about their allegiances, they might have reversed the order. The general merchandise store with all kinds of goods, although passé in the county seat, still enjoyed great favor in the backwoods towns. Store owners provided small loans necessary to sustain farmers and their families until their crops were harvested. They often owned farmlands themselves and would oblige a newcomer by setting him up on credit for land and mules. The store owner received his return for these services by charging high prices and interest rates. His economic services were supplemented by his valuable role in providing the community's social and educational centers. The owner and the men in the sun-faded overalls gathered whenever possible to polish off the community's history. Together they savored details about crops, ministers, sheriffs, morals, and family insurrections, which by collective confidentiality belonged only to the store's initiates and their close friends. Saturday nights sometimes provided an incident or two to add to the record. A man might walk into town to settle a grudge fight, to be witnessed by his son who walked respectfully behind him, or young men might drink too much and settle some issue of territoriality with knives as well as fists. Other nights, farmers, who had spare time during slack periods, drifted off peacefully to their houses before the store's lights were turned off, the official signal that everyone was to get ready for another day.

Greenwood, where Claude Neal lived, was located in gently sloping country about nine miles north of Marianna. In this farm-servicing town of approximately 1,300 inhabitants, there was

11. Jackson County *Floridan*, June 26, 1931, p. 5; Marianna *Daily Times-Courier*, June 9, 1932, p. 8.

only one private telephone in 1934. Greenwood and its immediate vicinity were noteworthy for a large black population which comprised about three-fourths of the town's numbers and an impressive count of independent black farmers who owned from forty to one hundred acres.[12] Some blacks were, of course, farm laborers such as Claude Neal; still others were croppers, tenants, and turpentine workers.

The county seat, Marianna, had undergone remarkable modernization in the 1920s. Its affluence with respect to the rest of the county was reflected in its size, 3,372 persons in 1930, its paved and well-lighted business section, and its numerous attractive houses.[13] It provided the nucleus for the county's trade, government and law, legal and medical services, and entertainment, especially movies. Farmers came to Marianna on Saturdays to buy and sell and to look around and watch progress. They drifted in and out, usually wearing overalls, talked politics in the vicinity of the courthouse, spat tobacco juice on the sidewalk and sized up the city folks. Insofar as they had a sense of belonging outside their farms, churches, and country stores, it was in the county seat.

The most distinguishing feature of Marianna was its gracious courthouse built in the early 1900s; its style was neoclassical, replete with an imposing cupola and broad, dignified columns (see Figure 1). Located on one of the community's modest hills, set off by shrubbery and antique oaks, and close to Confederate Park, it called attention to the traditionalism of the area. The business section close to the courthouse had its banks, stores, offices for two newspapers, automobile dealerships, barber and jewelry shops, many one-storied or at most, two (see Figures 2 and 3). Drugstores in the business area were favorite places to socialize. Girls gathered there late in the afternoon during the

12. *Sixteenth Census of the United States: 1940, Population, Vol. II, Pt. II,* 100; Chicago *Daily Tribune,* October 27, 1934, p. 1; Jackson County, Florida, Tax List (1934), available in County Courthouse, Marianna. This document lists six black families as owning forty acres or more.

13. *Florida State Census,* 1935, p. 91; Marianna Chamber of Commerce, *Marianna: The Hospitable City* (n.p., n.d.), in P. K. Yonge Library, University of Florida, Gainesville. On municipal improvements in Marianna in the 1920s see Jackson County *Floridan,* June 21, 1931, p. 10.

Fig. 1. Jackson County Courthouse in Marianna, Florida, as it appeared in the 1930s.

Courtesy of P. K. Yonge Library of Florida History, University of Florida, Gainesville, from pamphlet, *Marianna: Your Chance for Happiness and Profit* (Marianna Chamber of Commerce, n.d.)

summer, and the high school crowd occupied them during the school year. Blacks who came to the stores were prompt to enter, say what they wanted, and leave. The crowning triumph of Marianna's modernization in the 1920s came with construction of a five-story, fireproof hotel.[14] From its higher elevations an observer had a pleasant view of graceful, rolling woods and farmlands in every direction.

On the city's main street, adjacent to the business district, were several blocks of remarkably fine houses mostly in Geor-

14. Author's interview with John Winslett (local newspaper editor), September 26, 1977.

Fig. 2. View of Marianna, Florida, in the 1920s, in the vicinity of Jackson County Courthouse.

Fig. 3. Another view of Marianna, Florida, in the 1920s, in the vicinity of Jackson County Courthouse.

gian and plantation styles with spacious lawns and lovely gardens where the city's elite lived, especially its bankers, merchants, and professional persons. Women from this class sponsored the city's Little Theatre and Shakespeare Club, and their families sent sons and daughters respectively to the University of Florida and the Florida State College for Women. They held parties; they were the mainstays of those who celebrated the New Year's opening of the new hotel—the Chipola—in 1926 and had a great time

Courtesy of P. K. Yonge Library of Florida History, University of Florida, Gainesville, from pamphlet, *Marianna: Your Chance for Happiness and Profit* (Marianna Chamber of Commerce, n.d.)

Courtesy of P. K. Yonge Library of Florida History, University of Florida, Gainesville, from pamphlet, *Marianna: Your Chance for Happiness and Profit* (Marianna Chamber of Commerce, n.d.)

drinking and dancing despite prohibition.[15] Men and women from the town's upper class had traveled, were relatively sophisticated, and could be counted upon to call for community improvements.

The middle class of small store owners, teachers, ministers, artisans, and mechanics lived farther away from the downtown in more modest houses that more closely resembled one another.

15. Janie Smith Rhyne, *Our Yesterdays* (Marianna: n.p., 1968), 164.

They were less confident about their achievements, more traditional in viewpoint and conventional in behavior. There was
only a small white lower class in Marianna because blacks fulfilled its functions. The latter lived inconspicuously across the
railroad tracks but close enough to serve the white community
with laborers, maids, and yard boys.

Despite a progressive business class and superficial signs of
modernization, Marianna and the county which it served were
still old-fashioned southern places, relatively isolated from the
outside world as late as the 1920s. While Marianna was serviced
by a railroad and a handful of good roads, few residents owned
cars or traveled beyond their immediate area. In 1930 just three
in two hundred residents of the county subscribed to national
magazines, and in 1931 there were only three hundred telephone
subscribers among a population that exceeded thirty thousand.[16]

Since state and federal governments, in contrast with county
offices, were still abstractions for most county residents, this fact
reinforced the status quo mentality. While they built roads, cer-
tified teachers, maintained a public health officer, and operated a
post office and the federal district court, state and federal officials
did not establish a presence which modified attitudes or behavior; residents were much more concerned about the day-to-
day activities of the sheriff. And since he was assisted by only
two deputies in policing the large county, there was no sense in
trying to reach a sheriff thirty or forty miles away except for murders and bank robberies. On lesser issues, residents, who had
grown so accustomed to handling things themselves, might greet
him with, "What are you doing up here?" The overall effect of
this populist psychology was to resist change and reinforce local-
ism.[17]

While local business leaders invited comparison between Marianna's "present with just a few years ago" and the editor of one
of the local newspapers envisioned a golf course in his credo of
progress for the county, the poverty of many residents of the

16. Florida State Planning Board (ed.), *Statistical Abstract of Florida Counties,*
Jackson County (Jacksonville: Florida State Chamber of Commerce, 1944).
17. Author's interview with John Winslett, September 26, 1977.

county contrasted vividly with this type of boostering. Poor whites were as indigenous to the land of Jackson County as the cotton, peanuts, corn, sorghum, and potatoes they raised. Nearly half of the whites engaged in agriculture were either tenants or croppers (896 of 2,236 in 1930). Their income was considerably below the $970 averaged by Jackson County's independent cotton farmers in 1930 and the $890 averaged by other independent farmers with crop specialties.[18] For cotton, for example, assuming the cropper or tenant farmed an average of 30 acres and that he produced 150 pounds of cotton per acre, prices paid at the country store in Greenwood from 1925 through 1930 indicate that his earnings before debts would be only $700 a year.[19] By the time the farmer paid his shares, either a quarter or a half, and also the owner of the cotton gin for processing his cotton—usually a tenth of the crop—his cash income would be approximately $250 per year. Much of this would be consumed in debt at the country store. Since the acreage estimate is probably high, Vance declaring the average cotton acreage per farm reporting cotton to be only 12 acres in the Gulf Coast area, it is possible that the tenant's or sharecropper's income may have averaged between $100 to $200 per year.[20]

Surely, the numerous houses of these farmers still standing today are monuments to the gaunt survival of their earlier inhabitants. Many were then only one or two long rooms, although the better ones resembled those described by James Agee in *Let Us Now Praise Famous Men* with four rooms—two bedrooms, one for the children and one for the parents, a kitchen, and a parlor. Floors were bare, furniture sparse, rooms unlighted. The houses

18. Marianna *Floridan*, January 25, 1929, pp. 4, 11; *Statistical Abstract of Florida Counties*, Jackson County; *Fifteenth Census of the United States: 1930, Agriculture, Vol. III, Type of Farm, Pt. II*, 468.

19. Most farms where cotton was raised by poorer farmers had from 20 to 50 acres. See *Fifteenth Census of the United States: 1930, Agriculture, Vol. III, Pt. II*, 485. Prices on cotton per pound purchased were reviewed at the leading country store in Greenwood. On average they were 21 cents in 1925, 14 cents in 1926, 20 cents in 1927, 17 cents in 1928, 16 cents in 1929, and 9 cents in 1930. Records at Pender's Store, Greenwood, Florida.

20. Rupert B. Vance, *Human Factors in Cotton Culture: A Study in the Social Geography of the American South* (Chapel Hill: University of North Carolina Press, 1929), 235.

were vulnerable on every side, with leaks in the roof, holes in the wall, and crevices in the floors. They were hot in the summer when doors and windows were closed to keep out mosquitos and cold in the winter because the walls were not insulated and the single fireplace was wasteful of heat. When one couple was asked about the embarrassment of parents sleeping in the same room as children in those days, they laughed and said, "In the dark nobody knew the difference." But then one wonders how everyone felt about the sounds of old springs and bed frames. Regardless of the difficult lives of their parents, sons and daughters married young and for a while had the greatest adventure in their lives. And as the pleasures of the iron bed yielded children, nearly 15 percent of the county's population being five years or under in 1935, there were at least more and more hands for the field.[21]

Poor whites were seldom hungry though their diet was monotonous. Corn, largely consumed by animals, was also ground into meal to make corn bread. Sugarcane, grown in the vicinity of the farmer's house, produced a delicious syrup after its juice had been removed and cooked. Each farm family raised hogs, usually butchered in the winter when their meat was smoked and cured for a year. This process also provided lard which fried nearly every species of food served. There was also a "tater patch" and a field of perhaps an acre devoted to the raising of such vegetables as turnips, collards, green beans, squash, and black-eyed peas. Milk and eggs often were available though some families sold their eggs to obtain basic supplies. One of the great pleasures of this life for both body and soul was to eat a watermelon on a hot summer afternoon and fall asleep under a shade tree.

One source of food which also provided recreation for participants was the hunt. Men in Jackson County were especially fond of going into the woods with their alert hounds to shoot rabbit, quail, deer, and even squirrel. These excursions belonged exclusively to the men and the boys, who teamed with close friends in

21. Author's interview with Mr. C. and his wife, December 28, 1977; *Florida State Census*, 1935, pp. 68–69. Mr. C., who wishes to remain anonymous, was a young black man at the time of the Neal lynching.

a kind of fraternal foray, the game being carried home and given to the women for dressing and cooking. The hunt, which was basic to the experience of rural males in Jackson County, contributed to the psychology of stalking prey and doing so in the company of trusted friends, vital conditioning for the preparation of lynch parties.

The poor farmer's recreations were hardly more varied. Marianna was, of course, attractive, especially from October to Christmas, when he had money from his share of harvested crops. At these times or when attending a revival, he would wear socks and shoes and exchange his overalls and faded blue work shirt for a starched white shirt, trousers, and suspenders. His wife seldom had perfume or wore fancy underthings, but she might have a cotton print dress made at home from store material or a colorful flour sack and a few cheap ornaments for special times.

The poor white farmer's way of life was not merely devitalizing from the standpoint of poverty, monotony, and ignorance. He suffered the effects of diseases which also sapped his strength. The prevalence of swamps and the absence of screens made malaria the number one health problem in the county. Its chills and fever cut down the efficiency of all kinds of employment. Poor farmers were also plagued with pellagra, while their children, who went without shoes and were exposed to animal or human excrement, contracted hookworm. One federal survey among school children of the county in 1934 revealed that more than 80 percent had hookworm. Venereal diseases were apparently also present; a country store proprietor declared that in those days he sold large quantities of "Balsam Capiabia" for ten cents a bottle to cure its ravages.[22]

The white residents of this conservative, poor, and culturally isolated area displayed a social character molded by their frontier experiences, traditional values, and the dictates of white suprem-

22. Jackson County *Floridan*, September 14, 1934, p. 2; Florida State Board of Health, *Annual Report, 1936* (Jacksonville: Florida State Board of Health, 1937), 96–97. From a sample of 1,732 blood tests at clinics for venereal disease, 20 percent were positive. Interview of Walter Howard with Nick Pender, February 20, 1978.

acy. Those whites who settled the northern tier of Florida, including Jackson County, in the first two decades of the twentieth century were among the last American frontier men and women. They joined earlier residents who were themselves living in the spirit of the frontier with too few persons to tame that vast area. The slow economic development of Jackson County, especially its lack of cities, assured the perpetuation of frontier mores. Whites felt a moral right to do as they pleased ("You didn't need a permit to do anything") as long as they did not do injury to another.[23] And if they did, at least for the minor offenses, they expected to lose a few teeth. Government could do nothing but menace this type of freedom, and so issues were settled personally, if possible, to avoid contact with the law. Individualism keyed many other social forms. The local newspaper praised personal initiative and hard work; residents parked their cars in the middle of the street when there were no places on the curb; farmers refused to put up fences to keep livestock off the county roads; the moonshiner was a subculture hero.

One of the most disquieting features of this society's individualism was its lawlessness and continuous brinksmanship with violence. Citizens showed contempt for laws of government by refusing to pay taxes to vote and hunt. The supervisor of registration for elections in Jackson County informed Governor David Sholtz that less than half the voters in the state's important primary election were eligible because they had defaulted on poll taxes. She lamented, "Seems to me that Jackson County could have one *honest* election."[24] And the tax collector found it necessary to place a formal notice in the newspaper warning hunters that they would have to pay fees because "Governor Sholtz had advised prosecution of those who failed to secure licenses." Indeed, conditions had reached the stage where the local government seemed to question its own legitimacy. In one instance when ten charred gallon kegs containing liquor were seized by local officials, the mayor and chief of police, despite prohibition

23. Author's interview with Filmore Sims, September 27, 1977.
24. Mary Calhoun to Governor David Sholtz, October 20, 1934, in Jackson County Records, Florida State Archives, Tallahassee, Florida.

laws, presided over opening the kegs and allowing the liquor to run into an area where it could be consumed and bottled by the crowd.[25]

The inadequate number of county police officers invited lawlessness and vigilante violence. A careful reading of local newspapers suggests that an individual's survival in Jackson County, in the absence of effective civil authority, depended either on personal strength or on one's ability to get along with others. To cope with the situation most males owned guns. One elderly citizen recalls he was "raised in a county in which there was plenty of room and nearly everybody carried guns."[26] Although the local news editor was concerned about the increase in crime throughout the nation, he disapproved of gun control, which was, he thought, about as practical "as legislating against knives, automobiles and even iodine." There were numerous murders in the county, many for trivial reasons. Between November, 1933, and July, 1934, newspapers reported nine trials for murder or assault to commit murder. In one instance a man shot a policeman for hitting his son after arresting him for drunkenness, and in another a boy was shot while delivering papers by a man who suspected he was a chicken thief. In one bizarre episode, members of a family were hurling potatoes at one another when the husband of one of the participants rushed up with a pistol to protect his wife. He was killed and his wife wounded by her brother on the other side, who also had a pistol.[27]

In the absence of effective civil authority, nearly everyone was tempted to share power and to exercise it as his gun and impulse directed. Some persons, of course, especially women and blacks, were less equal than others in their potential to administer violence. As a consequence noblesse oblige characterized men's attitudes toward women.[28]

25. Marianna *Daily Times-Courier*, October 26, 1933, p. 6, January 7, 1932, p. 1.

26. Marianna *Floridan*, December 11, 1931, p. 1; Author's interview with Filmore Sims, September 27, 1977.

27. Marianna *Floridan*, November 11, 1931, p. 2, March 9, 1934, p. 1, April 20, 1934, p. 1; Marianna *Daily Times-Courier*, July 14, 1934, p. 1.

28. In the words of an especially informed commentator on Jackson County folkways in the 1930s, the former editor of one of the local newspapers, "Manli-

Evidence of disrespect for civil authority, of lawlessness and violence, suggests anarchy; but there were strong character-building influences which offset dangers of social fragmentation. The chief agencies for character formation, the family, schools, and churches, all operated along authoritarian lines and worked to produce agreeable personality types.

Families and schools in Jackson County prepared young people for life with firm no-nonsense codes of behavior. Person after person reared in this period recalls the disciplinary authority of his or her father. He was the unquestioned arbiter: "Where Poppa sat was the head of the table, no matter where he sat." Strict "yes and no sirs" and "yes and no ma'ams" were expected toward parents and elders at all times. Women were to be home because as one contemporary declared, "God made the woman for the man," but they too might administer punishment to children in the form of a preliminary spanking if the father were away from home. One elderly citizen recalled that he and his wife "wore out many switches on the children," and he believed that other families did the same thing. Lying to a parent automatically carried severe punishment in many families. Teachers didn't spare the rod either, and being sent to the superintendent was "like being condemned to death" because a second spanking awaited the scholar once he returned home.[29]

In the society at large adherence to strict standards of personal conduct (permits and promissory notes were equally objectionable), patriotism, love of the South, and Christian worship were all esteemed values which deserved unswerving allegiance. Men in the community celebrated the anniversary of the sinking of the *Maine*, and the entire community turned out for a mammoth parade honoring the two hundredth anniversary of the birth of George Washington. On that memorable occasion girls sang the "Washington Ode," and the speaker lauded Washington as the

---

ness was the key to the frontier spirit here. Men took care of women as part of that process. Girls didn't work. It was a sign of being taken care of." Author's interview with John Winslett, September 26, 1977.

29. Author's interviews with John Winslett, September 26, 1977, Filmore Sims, September 27, 1977, Roy Beale, December 27, 1977, and M. D. Cannidy, December 27, 1977.

first great military man in history since Genghis Khan to refuse a crown. The South and its gallant cause were also zealously guarded. When honors were extended the Confederate dead sixty-five years after the Civil War, a local editor declared that his county was "pregnant with the sweetest and holiest memories of the loved and lost cause" and for "the bravest and most gallant army the world has ever known."[30] The following year a band concert was dedicated to Robert E. Lee and the heroes of the battle of Marianna. Those who disagreed with these patriotic sentiments did not declare their opposition in the hometown, but when the local editor read about "debunking" historiography in other areas of the country, he righteously complained, "It gives us a deep-seated pain in the neck" because "there is nothing to be ashamed of in the history of America."[31]

Attendance at Christian worship and an outward profession of religious devotion were the most important ways to obtain social approval unless, of course, one also enjoyed wealth and power through business or inheritance. Men raised in the 1930s recall that Sunday was a very special day for starched shirts and plastered-down hair and mother's admonitions to hurry along with breakfast because the Sunday school bell would soon be ringing. The local newspapers served as similar tocsins for parents. Thus, the reminder near Christmas in an editorial: "By the way you know you should go to church every Sunday. Next Sunday is very important . . . your minister has a special message for you." The front-page message in August from the other local paper was similar: "Regardless of denomination, you should plan to attend at least one of the numerous devotional services on Sunday."[32]

Baptist and Methodist churches were numerically the strongest in Jackson County, though Marianna also had small congre-

30. Marianna *Daily Times-Courier*, February 11, 1932, p. 1, February 25, 1932, p. 1; Marianna *Floridan*, March 7, 1930, p. 4.

31. Jackson County *Floridan*, April 20, 1934, p. 2. Striking workers were also given short shrift. See editorial, "Make Them Work or Starve," in the *Floridan*, August 26, 1934, p. 2.

32. Author's interview with J. Earle Bowden, December 20, 1977; Marianna *Daily Times-Courier*, December 22, 1932, p. 2; Jackson County *Floridan*, August 25, 1933, p. 1.

gations of Adventists, Presbyterians, and Episcopalians.[33] The distinctions in religious services between Methodists and Baptists were negligible in Marianna, but both were more restrained in their religious enthusiasm than their counterparts in the smaller wooden churches in the country. Only prosperous merchants and professional people could afford the luxury of the song-sermon-prayer rituals of orderly religion. Poorer folks needed more dramatic victories over boredom and loneliness and so "footwashin' Methodists" and "shoutin' Baptists" attended country services on Wednesday nights and twice on Sundays. Everything was sweet and nice in those churches amidst good friends who related in a dramatic fashion their personal trials in looking for and finding God. And there were the attractive young women who apparently had a special talent for singing in the front row of the choir. Their pleasant faces and gentle swaying were also a source of general inspiration. None of the local ministers could equal, however, the emotional appeal of those traveling evangelists who often came to Jackson County. Real melodramatists, they sometimes held their meetings in the courthouse with the aid of publicity from an editorial in the local paper. One evangelist, J. A. Davis, promised to deliver talks entitled "Hear Them Red Hot Messages from the Book," "What I Would Do if I Were the Devil," "From Dance Hall to Hell," "Runaway Wife," and "Sermon to Men."[34]

Such pressures for conformity generated contempt for deviations. Those few who questioned the society's emphasis on religious values drew sharp criticism. Hence an editor's statement, "The *Floridan* sometimes receives a communication from some atheistic ass who wants a controversy. We have no room for such rot." Drunks in such a society inevitably became "sorry drunks," and the Democratic party was championed with the official sanction, "We love God, women and the Democratic Party in this old

33. Marianna *Daily Times-Courier*, October 8, 1931, p. 2. There were approximately 10,000 adults in all religious bodies in Jackson County in 1936. Of these 3,300 were Baptists and 3,700 Methodists, including both blacks and whites. See U.S. Department of Commerce, *Religious Bodies: 1936* (Washington, D.C.: U.S. Government Printing Office, 1941), Vol. I, 730–31.

34. Marianna *Daily Times-Courier*, April 7, 1932, p. 1, February 2, 1928, p. 3.

county."[35] Only once, when Alfred E. Smith, that abhorrent figure to orthodoxy, ran for president, did Jackson County deliver a substantial vote for a Republican presidential candidate.[36] Conformist attitudes and behavior among the local white population were best exemplified, however, in its relations with blacks.

Whites in Jackson County perceived blacks mainly in terms of their typical poverty, ignorance, and sycophantic behavior. Their assessment was probably not influenced by intimate knowledge of the personal lives of the black people with whom they dealt.[37] Whereas blacks knew much about the inner workings of white society as observers of their family and business lives, it would have been ignoble for whites to have similar knowledge. A member of the local intelligentsia commented on relations with blacks in the 1930s: "The last you would see of them was Friday night and on Monday morning you would be getting them out of jail, drunk." This absence of genuine communication is also underlined in a locally written novel depicting the lynching of Neal and the subsequent riot, when a black maid asks her white employers to drive her to "the quarters" despite threats by whites to burn the area. The white heroine is beside herself and asks, "Why doesn't she trust us? We've always been good to her."[38]

Competitive newspapers in a small community are probably a good reflection of community attitudes. There are few illustrations therein of overt racism. The general position taken in editorials and news stories is paternalistic toward helpful and harmless blacks and indifferent or hostile to the rest. Old-timey blacks were commended. They "had not forgotten to say Christmus Giff" at Christmastime, and they were proud to attend the funer-

35. Marianna *Floridan*, December 6, 1929, p. 5, November 27, 1931, p. 2; Author's interview with J. Earle Bowden, December 20, 1977.

36. Richard M. Scammon (ed.), *America at the Polls: A Handbook of American Presidential Election Statistics, 1920–1964* (Pittsburgh: University of Pittsburgh Press, 1965), 92–96. Hoover received 35.4 percent of the vote, more than twice the percentage given any other Republican candidate between 1920 and 1948.

37. Author's interview with John Winslett, September 27, 1977. See also a novel set in Marianna in the 1930s, M. E. Witherspoon, *Somebody Speak for Katy* (New York: Dodd and Mead, 1950), 45, where the protagonist concedes about Negroes, "I wonder what they're really like."

38. Witherspoon, *Somebody Speak for Katy*, 33.

als of their white benefactors and remark, "He sho was good ter me." Uncle Eli Harris, an antebellum Negro and fifty-year resident of Jackson County, was given a lifetime subscription to a local newspaper by the owner.[39] Similarly, a newspaper noted on its front page that blacks appreciated information which it had supplied on the importance of baths and keeping nails and feet clean. And when blacks performed as a musical quartet at an all-white festival, a newspaper columnist wrote, "The white folks here as elsewhere in the South, are always anxious to encourage the Negroes in every laudable work they may do, and hundreds here are doing much good work." Educated blacks who contributed to the community were respected, especially proponents of the Tuskegee ideal. Gilmore Academy in Marianna, which was committed to the goals of Booker T. Washington, was viewed in the local press as "a most creditable institution" and a "splendid force in the upbuilding of the colored race."[40]

Were it not for these occasional positive references to blacks, one would suspect from the newspapers that they comprised an insignificant community, not 40 percent of the county's population. When the killing of a black man occurred in a store owned by two white men, one of whom shot the black, the local news writer grieved, "The tragedy is regretted by friends of both the men," referring, however, only to the sad situation for the two store owners. Servants were disparaged because "nine-tenths of the local servants carry their meals home only to feed worthless, lazy members of their own families. And they refuse to work unless allowed the privilege of eating their meals at their own homes." Ads for a local dry cleaners employed Negro jokes. Negroes who quarreled were made to look ludicrous, and stories about them appeared on the front page along with stories headlined "Negroes Arrested on Booze Charge," or recounting arrests of blacks on charges of robbery or assault.[41]

39. Marianna *Floridan*, December 25, 1931, p. 2, February 14, 1930, p. 4; Marianna *Daily Times-Courier*, May 12, 1933, p. 5.
40. Marianna *Floridan*, March 23, 1928, p. 1, November 15, 1929, p. 2, May 16, 1930, p. 10.
41. Marianna *Daily Times-Courier*, July 25, 1928, p. 1, June 28, 1932, p. 1, February 23, 1928, p. 1; Marianna *Floridan*, October 2, 1931, p. 2; Jackson County

The perceptions blacks had of themselves and of their relation-ships with whites in Jackson County in the 1930s also convey a sense of their unimportance. It was commonly held in the black community of that period that if a black "had spunk he was crazy." There was "no way to stand up like a man." Some blacks felt they had no one willing to assist them when they opposed "the system" because they had no true friends in the white com-munity. Although upper-class whites might look upon them with "an eye of pity" as against hostile people in the lower classes, whites maintained solidarity on race issues. Furthermore, blacks could not conceive of asking for assistance from outside organi-zations like the NAACP. They felt cut off from the outside world and friendless there.[42]

Greater freedom for blacks today permits them to assert their frustrations about earlier times which could not have been ex-pressed then. Older blacks recall with some bitterness that they would "nurse white children to be knee high and then be forced to say 'mister' to the very children they had taken care of" while they became "Uncle" and "Auntie." Others remember how dan-gerous it was to be seen close to white women and how they would deliberately walk out of their way to avoid any chance of making contact with them. One man declared that Neal's fate could as easily have happened to any black man in Jackson County. Shopping in downtown clothing stores was often embar-rassing. Blacks were not allowed to try on clothing for fear it would lose value if the garments were then refused. Hats and shoes proved stubborn items to merchandise under the rule, how-ever, and so blacks were permitted to try on both as long as they laced their own shoes and wore tissue paper between hats and their heads.

Floridan, October 5, 1934, p. 7, January 5, 1934, p. 1; Author's interview with a group of Jackson County blacks, August 15, 1977.

42. Author's interviews with Mr. C., December 28, 1977, and with a group of Jackson County blacks, August 15, 1977. Blacks had little protection through vot-ing, of course, because of Florida's all-white Democratic primary. There were twenty-two blacks registered to vote in Marianna in the 1930s, most of them teachers, ministers, and carpenters. Voter Registration List, Jackson County Courthouse, Marianna.

Nearly every recollection by blacks of their social situation underscores their vulnerability. The large number of blacks who owned their own farms in Jackson County would seem to belie this fact. But blacks profess they held their farms on the good will of white bankers and moneylenders. They might "sacrifice morning to night, cradle to the grave and yet be busted." The banker or furnishing man could at any time move in and "even sweep the corn crib clean." Some blacks assert that he sometimes used underhanded tactics as well, such as not giving receipts for bales of cotton and then denying he received them. Hence, even independent black farmers got "older by the year worrying." Many of them took on a second job as a laborer. It was said about them that they worked for "a hog's head," *i.e.*, the undesirable remains of a butchered hog, the recompense for their extra work for whites. Similarly, blacks declare they tried to avoid involvements with the police and the courts because they felt that they would be treated unjustly. One man illustrated the problem by saying that if a car owned by a white man ran into the car of a black man, the police officer would walk up to the black man and say, "Hey boy, what are you going to do?" Everyone knew that the situation would be reversed in the courts. Black women were also vulnerable. Black men concede there was no way to protect them then, but acknowledge that most white men did not take advantage of their opportunities. Blacks even lacked guns at the time, so their defenselessness was complete. The one exception, according to a black who lived in the 1930s, occurred when blacks lived in the same place as whites as their servants or tenants and then only if they stayed in their place at all times. They might then enjoy protection if their offenses were not grave.[43]

Blacks reacted to discrimination by withdrawal and found gratifications among themselves. There were church picnics, guitar "pickin's," and swims in a special place on the Chipola River. And in their churches, in cleaner pairs of overalls, they poured out torrents of feelings during the services, deriving satisfaction

43. Author's interview with a group of Jackson County blacks, August 15, 1977.

from the thought that "things would not be the same, next time around."[44]

The Depression, coupled with the innovative policies of the New Deal, produced severe social tensions in Jackson County; these increased the likelihood of mob violence against blacks. The Depression brought devastating losses in farm income, foreclosures, and very large numbers of rural unemployed. By October, 1933, Jackson County had the second largest number of rural persons (8,290) on relief for any county in Florida.[45] Conditions were so bad that the bank in Graceville, Florida (Jackson County), the state's largest cotton-producing center, was forced to close. One exceptionally well informed resident speculated that 80 percent of the county's farmland could be purchased for taxes during the Depression era. A man employed as a rural mail carrier at the time remembers that while farmers had food they didn't have money to send letters.[46]

Although the New Deal's policies through 1934 helped the local economy, they also created trouble spots for a tradition-bound society. Although the local newspaper editor lauded the New Deal for organizing crop production, thereby assuring profit for owners, he expressed concern about the effects of unemployment relief on the character of dispossessed farmers and tenants. He was appalled that the government employed "destitute persons on a dole," declaring "needy people can best be relieved through education and training and in a spirit of self-reliance which is sadly lacking today."[47] Large landowners in the county shared these misgivings; they feared the New Deal's relief programs would undermine their social and economic power. How could

44. Author's interview with Mr. C., December 28, 1977.
45. There were 8,987 people on relief rolls in Jackson County in October, 1933, of which 8,290 were rural population. In Florida only Escambia County, with a much larger population, had a greater number of its rural population unemployed. See Federal Emergency Relief Administration, "Unemployment Relief Census," Florida File, National Archives, Washington, D.C. The economy of towns in Jackson County suffered, of course, as agricultural income plummeted.
46. Marianna *Floridan*, June 26, 1931, p. 5; Author's interviews with John Winslett, November 10, 1977, and Filmore Sims, September 27, 1977.
47. Jackson County *Floridan*, September 28, 1934, p. 4. See also the *Floridan* for December 8, 1933, p. 2, and November 30, 1934, p. 1.

they continue to set wage scales or control attitudes towards work if the government offered thirty cents an hour for work relief?[48] In Greenwood, landowners complained that "those on relief did not need all they were getting and besides it was falling in the wrong hands anyhow."[49]

Government relief programs were a mixed blessing for small farmers as well. The net result of the AAA's complicated programs calling for voluntary reduction of cotton assured the income of large landowners (cotton prices were twelve cents per pound in Jackson County in 1933, up from five cents per pound in 1929), but reduced the need for tenants, who either went on relief or became casual laborers.[50] Relief benefits from federal programs such as CWA and FERA could not compensate former farm operators fully for the loss of their farms or their right to work for shares; the damage was psychological and the cost, shrunken self-esteem. This may account for the sensitivity of those on relief to real or imagined slights from local administrators, who were usually from prominent local families. Relief recipients in Jackson County, Florida, formed the FERA Purification League and attacked local administrators of federal programs as a self-serving political clique.[51] They even forwarded an appeal to President Roosevelt, signed by 1,100 persons in the county, denouncing the "secretiveness, evasiveness and discourtesy" which allegedly characterized local relief operations.

Blacks might easily become the target of the collective frustrations among whites during this period of rapid social change. A surprisingly large number of black farmers owned their own farms (410, one-fourth of all black farmers in Jackson County) in

48. The views of the large landowning farmers are presented in editorals in the Jackson County *Floridan*, December 8, 1933, p. 2, and September 7, 1934, p. 4. The editor viewed with apprehension "the numbers employed on civil works projects . . . which is resulting in a shortage of the type of labor necessary for production and processing of the products of the farm." Note the editor's pleasure when the federal wage rate is dropped (see issue of December 7, 1939, p. 4).

49. *Ibid.*, September 7, 1934, p. 4.

50. On cotton prices see Jackson County *Floridan*, August 31, 1934, p. 2. Jackson County cotton growers received more than $40,000 to plow up 3,500 acres of the crop in 1933.

51. Jackson County *Floridan*, September 27, 1934, p. 1.

1930 or were cash tenants, and they were aided by the Farm Credit Administration during the 1930s.[52] Since many whites were landless in-migrants from other states or dispossessed sharecroppers, the economic strength of these blacks confounded the society's normal reward system. Whites on relief may have resented blacks because they were competing with them for federally funded jobs or because they assumed Negroes preferred to receive relief money for doing no work. The difference in average weekly income between relief workers ($11.70) and those on non-working direct relief ($7.61), therefore, might have seemed unjust to them. Animosities between this group and blacks had reached the point in October, 1934, that the FERA Purification League was reportedly preparing a demonstration to purge black relief recipients from FERA rolls. Needless to say, acute competition developed between blacks and whites for the few jobs that were available, and the entire situation created an ominous background for mob violence against blacks.[53]

52. *Statistical Abstract of Florida Counties*, Jackson County. Only 13.1 percent of black farmers owned their own farms in the South overall. Gunnar Myrdal, Richard Sterner, and Arnold Rose, *An American Dilemma: The Negro Problem and Modern Democracy* (New York: Harper and Row, 1944), 236. Forty-six black farmers in Jackson County received loans from the Farm Credit Administration in a three-month period in 1934. See Records of Farm Credit Administration, "Crop Mortgages," Jackson County Courthouse, Marianna.

53. Jackson County *Floridan*, September 28, 1934, pp. 1, 10; Tallahassee *Democrat*, November 3, 1935, p. 1; Howard Kester, "The Marianna, Florida Lynching," 12–13, in Lynching File, Series 278, Florida State Archives, Tallahassee.

Chapter 3

The Suspect

"One of the most horrible crimes in Jackson County's history was brought to light with the discovery on last Friday morning [October 19, 1934] of the mutilated body of Miss Lola Cannidy, nineteen year old Jackson County girl, on a wooded hillside near her home about three and one-half miles northeast of Greenwood."[1] The murdered girl was a daughter of Mr. and Mrs. George Cannidy, the youngest daughter of their eight children. The Cannidy family lived in a primitive four-room house, marked by a weathered clapboard exterior with a galvanized roof.[2] The Cannidys were industrious country folks, "hard working and honest," the basic compliment poor farmers paid one another in this impoverished agricultural area of northwest Florida. Lola was a petite, attractive girl who was engaged to be married to a young man from a nearby community. Remembered by contemporaries as a "sweet child," "always smiling," and a "nice girl," who was five feet tall and weighed eighty to ninety pounds, she was clearly a family favorite.[3]

1. Jackson County *Floridan*, October 26, 1934, p. 1.
2. The Cannidy house was typical for poor Jackson County farmers of their day. A number of these houses still stand today. Interview of author and Walter Howard with M. D. Cannidy, December 30, 1977.
3. Interview of author and Walter Howard with John Winslett, September 17, 1977; Author's interview with Nick Pender, December 15, 1977; Interviews of author and Walter Howard with Roy Beall, December 27, 1977, and M. D. Cannidy, December 30, 1977.

The day Lola Cannidy was murdered, most of her family had gone to visit one of her adult brothers, leaving her and a seven-year-old brother, who was playing in the fields, at the homestead. She was apparently ironing clothes when she decided to leave the house about noon, Thursday, October 18, to walk several hundred yards through an open field to a pump where hogs were watered. When the family returned and Lola did not appear even as darkness approached, they began to search for her. That night several friends and neighbors joined them with guns, dogs, and lanterns; they fanned out through the fields behind the Cannidy house where black families, who worked the fields and did odd jobs in the area, lived. Many curious neighbors began to assemble at the Cannidy farm to see what was happening. At 6:30 the following morning, as Sheriff Flake Chambliss arrived, a Cannidy relative spotted a discarded shoe under a bush and then the crudely hidden body of the young woman.[4] The searchers were sickened by what they saw under two large logs and a pine bough cover. Lola Cannidy had been beaten to death with a bloodied hammer used for fence repair, which had been left in the Cannidy field earlier; her head was pulverized. Her body was "fully clothed," except for her shoes and hat. She had been dragged only a short distance from the spot where she had fought her assailant.[5]

After viewing the body, Sheriff Chambliss permitted the family to carry Lola's remains home for inspection by the county physician and to make preparation for her funeral; her father, George, insisted on cradling her crushed head in his lap during the brief trip.

The frightened, angry crowd provided the sheriff with rumors of suspicious persons. The sheriff's report, later filed with Florida Governor David Sholtz, reveals that he received no convincing

---

4. Interview of author and Walter Howard with M. D. Cannidy, December 30, 1977; Sheriff W. Flake Chambliss to Governor David Sholtz, October 21, 1934, in Official Correspondence of Governor David Sholtz, Florida State Archives, Tallahassee; Jackson County *Floridan*, October 26, 1934, p. 1.

5. Marianna *Daily Times-Courier*, October 23, 1934, p. 1; Interview of author and Walter Howard with Roy Beall, December 30, 1977. Roy Beall searched the fields for Lola's murderer and recalls the appearance of the area where the struggle occurred.

information about strangers in that backcountry area that Thursday afternoon.[6] His attention turned to two local men who apparently had disappeared at that time: Calvin Cross, a white, and Claude Neal, a black. It was reported to Sheriff Chambliss that Neal, who lived on a bluff within a quarter mile of the Cannidy home in Greenwood, had gone into a field close to the water pump just after his dinner at noon, returned about two hours later, and then left home for the night. It is also probable that Sheriff Chambliss heard tales about Neal's hands looking "skinned up." At any rate, the sheriff ordered Neal arrested on suspicion within two hours after he had viewed the scene of the crime. Neal was found in a corncrib at his employer's nearby farm, where he had spent the night after first having requested permission to do so.[7] The sheriff's diary of events on Friday, October 19, recorded what evidence and information he found:

6:00 A.M.:   Sheriff notified of missing girl.
6:30 A.M.:   Body of girl found in woods about one-eighth of a mile southeast of water pump, with head crushed.
6:45 A.M.:   Sheriff views body in woods; and finds piece of cloth near body, which was fitted into Neal's shirt that night.
8:30 A.M.:   Coroner's jury impanelled.
8:30 A.M.:   Neal arrested on suspicion by Deputy Coulliette and brought to Marianna. He was transferred immediately to Chipley where he remained about an hour, and was then transferred to Panama City. When arrested, his watch ring was out of his watch.
9:00 A.M.:   Watch ring found in woods near where body was found, and turned over to Sheriff that night.
9:30 A.M.:   Dr. Hodges [county physician] makes examination of body for coroner's jury, and reports that she had been murdered—that she was bruised and lacerated.
10:00 A.M.:   Sallie Smith, great aunt of Neal, arrested by Sheriff and placed in Chipley [Florida]; and Neal's wet clothes were taken from her house. She and Neal lived in same house.

6. Sheriff W. Flake Chambliss to Governor David Sholtz, October 31, 1934, in Lynching File, Series 278, Florida State Archives; Interview of author and Walter Howard with M. D. Cannidy, December 30, 1977.
7. Interview of author and Walter Howard with Roy Beall, December 30, 1977; Chambliss to Sholtz, October 31, 1934, in Lynching File, Series 278, Florida State Archives.

11:00 A.M.:	Tracks of two persons along North and South fence discovered. One looked like a man's track and the other like a woman's track. Reported to Sheriff at 1:00 P.M.
12:00 Noon:	Dr. MacKinnon [another local physician] makes examination of body at request of Sheriff and State Attorney, and reports no signs of rape appear. . . .
3:00 P.M.:	Checked up on whereabouts of white man named Calvin Cross, who was under suspicion, and absolved him.
4:00 P.M.:	Lola Cannidy buried at Bascom [Florida].[8]

The evidence against Neal was not fully convincing, though it was sufficient to make him a prime suspect. The piece of bloodied cloth which the sheriff alleged fit Neal's torn shirt surely warranted careful scrutiny, as did the bloody clothes reportedly found in his shack. The extensive cuts on Neal's hands, observed by several persons, were not explained by him in a consistent manner. His employer testified before the coroner's jury that Neal told him that he had received the cuts while fixing a fence. A Negro and a white youth testified that they saw Neal Thursday night before sundown and that he told them his cuts came from fighting.[9] Only moments later, however, he reportedly told them his cuts occurred when he jumped over a barbed-wire fence. Parenthetically, a black who lived in the same area as Neal recalled one of his older relatives describing Neal about sunset, Thursday: "I saw Claude Neal walk by. He had a strange look and his hands was all cut up. I believe he done killed Miss Lola."[10]

The other evidence against Neal at the time was less persuasive. No tests were made to determine whether Neal's fingerprints were on the murder weapon. The watch ring discovered near the scene of the murder was "fitted" into Neal's pocket watch which had a missing ring; but no one could establish that Neal had recently lost the ring to his watch, and such rings were

8. Chambliss to Sholtz, October 31, 1934, in Lynching File, Series 278, Florida State Archives.

9. Howard A. Kester, "The Marianna, Florida Lynching," 7, Lynching File, Series 278, Florida State Archives; Marianna *Daily Times-Courier*, October 23, 1934, pp. 1, 4.

10. Interview of author and Walter Howard with confidential source, August 15, 1977.

generally standard, after all.[11] Though allegations were made that Neal's mother, with whom Neal lived, and his aunt had washed his bloody clothes, both had been spirited out of town by the sheriff, who feared they might be harmed, and neither testified before the coroner's jury. His sister, a thirteen-year-old, told the coroner's jury that Neal's clothes had been washed that night, but they were not bloody.[12] The next day from the Chipley jail, Neal's mother admitted washing his clothes after he came back to the house from the field and said there was blood on them. She did so, however, while being held in jail, only one hour after a mob had demanded the two women and had threatened to come back and dynamite the jail. Finally, a few people in the community believed Neal guilty because he and Lola had been seen talking together.[13] If true, this circumstance could be explained by the fact that Lola Cannidy and Claude Neal had played together as children and had known one another nearly all their lives. It was not uncommon in the South for black and white children to play together when their families lived close to one another. Association between boys and girls of the two races terminated when they reached puberty, but Lola and Claude may have seen one another occasionally thereafter because several blacks, including Neal, worked for the Cannidys, and Lola reportedly visited Neal's older relatives.[14]

In this country in the deep South in the 1930s it was unnecessary to establish a motive for the slaying of a pretty white girl when a Negro male was suspect. In the minds of most white men of that period the nearest thing to heaven for a Negro male was to have a white girl. Besides, one physician testified that Lola had

11. There is no suggestion of confirmatory evidence from newspapers or the sheriff's report that the watch ring belonged to Neal's watch. These merely make mention of the fact that Neal's watch lacked a ring and a ring was discovered near Miss Cannidy's body.

12. Marianna *Daily Times-Courier*, October 23, 1934, p. 4. According to a black who was related to Neal's family, Neal was not living with his wife at the time of his arrest. Interview of author and Walter Howard with confidential source, August 15, 1977.

13. Chambliss to Sholtz, October 31, 1934, in Lynching File, Series 278, Florida State Archives; Jackson County *Floridan*, October 26, 1934, p. 8.

14. Interview of author and Walter Howard with confidential source, September 27, 1977; Author's interview with Nick Pender, December 15, 1977.

been raped. It was unthinkable that the white girl's death might have resulted from anger over a broken love relationship. Yet a gifted commentator, a southern, white liberal, who conducted a week-long investigation of the complex episode for the NAACP shortly after its occurrence, believed that Neal might have killed Lola Cannidy because he was a spurned lover. Howard A. Kester reported:

> Neal had played with the Cannidy children and when he was large enough to work, worked on the Cannidy farm. For some months and possibly for a period of years, Claude Neal and Lola Cannidy had been having intimate relations with each other. The nature of their relationship was common knowledge in the Negro community. Some of his friends advised him of the danger of the relationship and had asked him not to continue it. Miss Cannidy, it seems, desired to break the relationship existing between herself and Neal and the fatal meeting was prearranged for the purpose of arriving at some understanding. At the meeting in the woods, Miss Cannidy told Neal that she did not want him to speak to her again and that if he did so, she would tell the white men in the community on him. (Should Miss Cannidy have told on him it would mean certain death.) When she told Neal that she wanted to quit and further threatened to "tell on him," he "got mad and killed her." Neal later told a friend what had happened. Neal is reported to have told the friend, "When she said she didn't want me to speak to her and then told me that she'd tell the white men on me, I just got mad and killed her."[15]

Although Kester supplied an additional motive for the murder, he was not totally convinced that Neal had killed Lola ("I still have some doubts in my mind") and therefore was dubious about his own explanation for the crime. As might be expected, Kester's allegations, however tentative, were heatedly denied in Jackson County and are denied to this day among whites who knew Lola Cannidy well, especially her family and friends.[16]

In the minds of many blacks, law enforcement officials broke off their search for other suspects prematurely. As a socially ineffectual and inarticulate group, extremely frightened in the aftermath of Lola Cannidy's murder, the county's blacks confined

15. Kester, "The Marianna, Florida Lynching," 6–7.
16. Interviews of author and Walter Howard with James Kane (a member of Cannidy family), December 29, 1977, and with Roy Beall, December 28, 1977.

their displeasure to complaints among themselves. Kester had heard rumors in the black community that a white man murdered Miss Cannidy and took his bloodstained clothes to Neal's house and asked his mother to wash them, presumably for money. But Kester declared he was "unable to find any substantial support for the theory among Negroes in the [Greenwood] community."[17] He believed they might have been too frightened to discuss the subject with him. Rumors, however, circulated among blacks themselves. Proof is a letter to an NAACP official from a black minister in a community about fifty miles from Greenwood:

> It was reported that clothes with blood stains on them were found at Neal's home. . . . It is said that the white man who killed the white girl in question sent those clothes to Neal to be washed by his mother. . . . These may or may not be facts but they deserve investigation. Living as I do where it is dangerous for me or any other man of color to write or say too much . . . I am giving you a hint of some things being said here.[18]

To this day blacks in Jackson County are divided on the question of Neal's guilt.[19] Slightly more emboldened over forty years after the incident, they often respond simply with the comment, "Some say yes and some say no" (substitute "Some say yes but most feel or want to feel no"). Some blacks allege that a white resident of Malone, Florida, made repeated confessions to the crime. After murdering Miss Cannidy he supposedly paid Neal to exchange clothes with him. Although many blacks accept this story and believe that it exonerates Neal, it is impossible to find data to substantiate this account. A combination of fright among local blacks over the incident, helplessness before the police and the courts, and ignorance of methods of documentation could explain the absence of verifiable data.

17. Author's interview with several blacks in Jackson County, August 17, 1977; Kester, "The Marianna, Florida Lynching," 8.
18. Rev. C. M. Carson to William Pickens, November 5, 1934, NAACP Papers, C-352, Manuscript Division, Library of Congress.
19. Author's interview with a group of seven blacks from Jackson County, August 14, 1977. All were old enough to recall circumstances of the Cannidy murder and Neal lynching. All stressed they wished to remain anonymous.

Despite the fact that evidence at the time appeared insufficient to determine Neal's guilt beyond reasonable doubt, and even before the coroner's jury charged Neal on the basis of its one-day review of evidence, lynch mobs were speeding down the roads of northwest Florida looking for him.[20] Jackson County residents surrounded Sheriff Chambliss' home and demanded to know where Neal was being kept.[21] Several members of the crowd, which included women, had guns. A large segment of the white community was enraged: guns were everywhere, in the backs of automobiles and in hip holsters and inside men's coats. One young man in his car shouted to pedestrians in Marianna, "We've got him!" Within minutes, cars came from every direction as if to join a lynch party; it was only by daring driving down county roads that he and his friends were able to elude their pursuers.[22]

Descriptions in local newspapers of the burial of the young woman and statements by bereaved members of her family turned anger into conviction that Neal was the murderer. On Saturday, October 20, the *Floridan* carried on its front page comments by members of the Cannidy family. Under a column headed, "You Can't Know How It Hurts Unless This Happens to You," Lola's father was quoted as saying:

> Lord, but you can't know how it hurts unless you had something like this happen to someone you loved. . . . The bunch have promised me that they will give me first chance at him when they bring him back and I'll be ready. We'll put those two logs on him and ease him off by degrees. I can't get the picture of Lola out of my mind when we found her. Her throat was bruised and scratched where he had choked her so she couldn't cry out. My son was in the field about a quarter of a mile away when he saw someone talking with her at the pump, but he thought it was just one of the local boys and didn't pay much attention. He was right there in the field when she was being killed. Her head was beat in and she had been choked so hard her eyes were com-

20. Chambliss to Sholtz, October 31, 1934, in Lynching File, Series 278, Florida State Archives.

21. Interview of author and Walter Howard with M. D. Cannidy, December 30, 1977. On hostility faced by the sheriff for withholding information on Neal's whereabouts, see letter of his neighbor, J. D. Smith, to Governor David Sholtz, November 2, 1934, in Lynching File, Series 278, Florida State Archives.

22. Interview of author and Walter Howard with Arthur Jensen, December 20, 1977.

ing out of their sockets, her arms were broken and she was all beat up. When I get my hands on that nigger, there isn't any telling what I'll do.[23]

Lola's sister was quoted in a headline for another front-page column titled, "I Wish Every Resident of Jackson County Could See the Body of Lola." She too expressed disbelief at the enormity of the crime and called for vengeance against Claude Neal, whom she assumed had attacked her sister.

> When I viewed the body of my sister I was horrified. Whoever killed her—well I don't believe any form of punishment could fit the crime. I can hardly believe that such a horrible thing could happen to my sister. If I have to be killed I hope it won't be in the manner she met death. I know that there never has been anything in Jackson County that was so brutal. I'd just like to see the man who did this just once. I can't understand what the motive was for this brutal deed. To think that Claude Neal, who had been raised with my sister and me and worked for us all his life, could do such a thing—it is unbelievable. I only wish that every resident of Jackson County could view the body of my sister. If they could, they wouldn't rest until the murderer was caught and justice meted out.[24]

Grim-faced men outside the courthouse, in the American Legion Club, in the country stores, and along the red clay roads talked that week about only one subject, the sweet girl and her brutal black assailant. They recalled that she was the prettiest girl you ever saw and had always helped out at home. The Cannidys might have been relatively poor, but they were good people and always worked hard. What a shame for them to lose a nice daughter. And the way her face was all smashed in. And to think she was engaged and had her whole life before her. Girls all over the county had to do chores in the fields. How could the white men protect them from things like this? You couldn't trust the "niggers" to keep their hands off a decent white girl if you turned around. The best thing in the world for them is to have a white girl. To think that the family knew that "nigger" and was friendly with him nearly all his life. There was no way you could trust

23. Marianna *Daily Times-Courier*, October 20, 1934, p. 1.
24. *Ibid.*

them with white women. A couple years back a Negro boy thought about raping a white girl and got scared and gave it up, and the boys up in Greenwood knew they would have to put the fear of God in him. They took him out each afternoon for a week and just beat the tar out of him.[25] Where would it stop with the "niggers" if the white men didn't teach them a lesson over something like this?

The fact that Neal had a bad reputation among local whites clinched the verdict against him. He is remembered by several whites, some of whom profess they knew him well, and one black who was raised close to him, as a "mean nigger." Several whites declared he was "uppity," "insolent," and "overbearing," and one noted he was "overindulged" by his aunt, who played an important role in his raising.[26] The same person asserted, "He wasn't afraid of anything, not a single thing." He contends that he first suggested to Sheriff Chambliss that Neal be considered a suspect for the murder after he heard of Lola's death and the cuts on Neal's hands because Neal was "even mean with his own people and was in trouble all the time."[27]

At nine o'clock on Monday morning, October 22, before Neal had made a confession, a coroner's jury at the county courthouse in Marianna completed its investigation into the death of Lola Cannidy. Given the embittered feelings of many whites, its report was an incitement to violence against Neal. Before "a large number of spectators who jammed every possible space" the jury found that:

> Lola Cannidy, in the peace of God; then and there being feloniously and willfully, with malice aforethought [raped] and that the said Claude Neal with a certain blunt instrument which he then and there held in and upon said Lola Cannidy, did inflict a mortal wound. . . . That the said Claude Neal, in the manner aforesaid, did then and there

25. Interview of author and Walter Howard with Arthur Jensen, December 20, 1977.
26. Interviews of author and Walter Howard with four confidential sources who affirmed this view of Neal in separate interviews, August 15–December 29, 1977.
27. Interview of author and Walter Howard with a confidential source, December 28, 1977.

kill and murder, and said jurors do further say, upon their oath afore-said, that Annie Smith and Sallie Smith were feloniously present at the time of the felony and murder aforesaid in manner committed . . . comforting, aiding and abetting the said Claude Neal to do so and commit the said felony and murder.[28]

More than three hundred residents of Jackson County had al-ready been tracking Neal, his aunt, and his mother for two days by the time the coroner's jury delivered its account. At seven o'clock the previous Friday evening, one of Sheriff Chambliss' two deputies phoned him that "suspicious looking cars" were moving in the direction of nearby Chipley, where Neal's mother and aunt were in the Washington County jail, and toward Pan-ama City, about sixty miles from Marianna, where Neal was being kept in the Bay County jail.

The sheriff's chronicle records that he took precautions to pro-tect the rights of Neal and the two women and attempted to keep their whereabouts a secret. An entry for 4:30 P.M., Saturday, stated: "Proposition to Sheriff that if he will cut down size of guard transporting Neal after conviction the mob would probably let him be brought to trial, flatly refused."[29]

The mob began its probe of jails within a seventy-five-mile ra-dius of Marianna on Friday night. The Chipley *Banner* described "a crowd of Jackson County citizens who came in looking for a negro who murdered a Miss Cannidy near Greenwood. After being assured he was not here the crowd faded away. However, the officers had a few anxious moments of not knowing what might be expected." Saturday night a band of approximately three hundred men returned and threatened to dynamite the Chipley jail unless Sheriff John Harrell turned over the "negro suspects" to them. The sheriff had requested from the governor's office and received tear-gas bombs which he vowed to use if the mob at-tempted to break into the jail.

At daybreak Sunday morning, October 21, a crowd of men again came to the Chipley jail, this time with acetylene torches,

28. Marianna *Daily Times-Courier*, October 23, 1934, pp. 1, 4.
29. Chambliss to Sholtz, October 31, 1934, in Lynching File, Series 278, Florida State Archives.

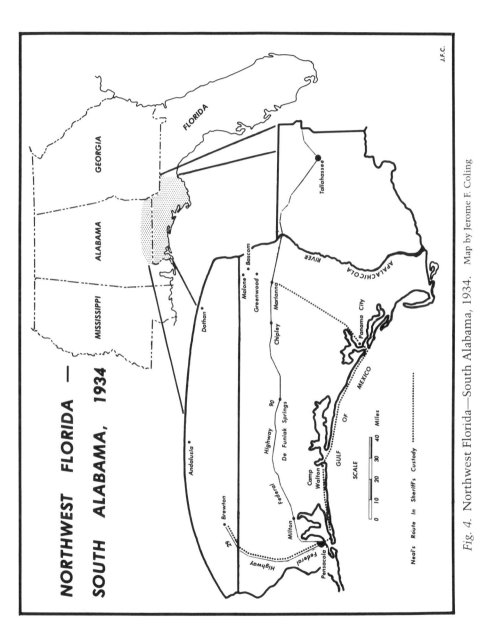

Fig. 4. Northwest Florida—South Alabama, 1934. Map by Jerome F. Coling

to cut their way through the cell block to seize Neal's mother and aunt. Sheriff Harrell feared there was insufficient tear gas on hand to disperse the mob so he decided to drive the women to Pensacola. He hid the two on the floor of his automobile and drove carefully through the mob-filled streets and out of Chipley and westward to Pensacola. According to the sheriff, the mob in Chipley was armed with knives and guns, some of them were drinking, and others were pleading with him through tears to release the two black women to them.[30]

Although the Panama City *Pilot* reported that Neal arrived in Panama City about 6:00 P.M. on Friday, October 19, Sheriff Chambliss' chronicle implies that Neal may already have been there early Friday afternoon.[31] The mob's pursuit was hot and relentless. They reached the Bay County jail about 9:30 P.M., only half an hour after Neal had been removed by boat to Camp Walton, Florida (now Fort Walton Beach), and then to Pensacola by automobile. The *Pilot* captured the mob's solemn mood as well as the widespread sympathy for its members in the vicinity of the crime; lawmen took care not to provoke those bent on lynch murder.

> The mob was over 100 men, in the 27 cars, unmasked, composed largely of farmers. It reached Panama City at 9:30 and went directly to the jail demanding the Negro. The jailer . . . told them that Sheriff Hobbs had left with the Negro and he did not know where they were headed for. The jailer then allowed leaders of the mob to make a complete search of the jail and premises.
>
> When the Negro was not found, the crowd still waited around the jail. Sheriff Hobbs had returned then and explained to the crowd that he had been requested to remove the Negro by the officers of Jackson County, and that the Negro was then out of Bay County. He asked the men kindly to disperse and expressed deepest sympathy for them.
>
> The crowd of Jackson countians were orderly, quiet and determined, talking in undertones. None were masked. There was no display of

30. Chipley *Banner*, October 25, 1934, p. 1; Washington County *News*, October 25, 1934, p. 1; Panama City *Pilot*, October 25, 1934, p. 1. For mob reactions in Chipley, see Pensacola *Journal*, October 22, 1934, p. 1.
31. Chambliss to Sholtz, October 31, 1934, in Lynching File, Series 278, Florida State Archives.

arms, no boisterousness. They were 100 men determined to defend womanhood against a crime.[32]

Sheriff Herbert E. Gandy of Escambia County brought Claude Neal into Pensacola in the early hours of Saturday morning, October 20. Gandy was apprehensive about keeping Neal in the Escambia County jail, which was about 140 miles west of Marianna, because a band of vigilantes had attempted to storm it for Neal the previous night and the jail was regarded as too flimsy to withstand attack.[33] He persuaded an army police unit then garrisoned at Fort Barrancas located on the Pensacola Naval Air Station to accept Neal for several hours. Then Gandy decided to remove the prisoner to Brewton, an Alabama town fifty-five miles north of Pensacola for safe keeping. Although adjacent counties in Alabama and Florida had followed this practice of lodging prisoners, Gandy's decision was most unfortunate for Neal, who would have been safer in the detention facility at Fort Barrancas or even in Mobile, which was only slightly farther than Brewton from Pensacola. Neal's mother and aunt had been removed to Fort Barrancas, where they remained safe after threats to their lives at Chipley.[34] In addition, Brewton's jail was dilapidated and protected by only a small police force.[35]

When Gandy appeared in Brewton at daybreak on Saturday morning, he pleaded with Sheriff G. A. Byrne of Escambia County, Alabama, to keep Neal for a day or two.[36] He told Byrne

32. Panama City *Pilot*, October 25, 1934, pp. 1, 6.

33. Gandy's concern over the adequacy of the jail in Pensacola and his placing Neal temporarily at Fort Barrancas are recorded in the Birmingham *News*, October 26, 1934, p. 1.

34. Chambliss to Sholtz, October 31, 1934, in Lynching File, Series 278, Florida State Archives.

35. A report on the poor condition of the Brewton jail followed the seizure of Neal. See Glenn Andrews, State Prison Inspector, to Board of County Commissioners, Escambia County, Alabama, November 8, 1934, in Escambia County Courthouse, Brewton, Alabama.

36. Interview of Hugh M. Caffey with Sheriff G. S. Byrne. Caffey, on instructions of Alabama Governor B. M. Miller, investigated the seizure of Neal at Brewton, making an effort to talk to all Alabamians who had firsthand knowledge of the event. The interviews were conducted from November 1 to November 5, 1934. They may be found in the Governor B. M. Miller Papers, Alabama State Archives, Montgomery.

that mobs were determined to lynch Neal and asked him to provide temporary sanctuary in order to see "if they might be able to
get a confession from him." Sheriff Byrne agreed and the two
sheriffs pledged they would keep Neal's whereabouts secret. He
was booked as John Smith from Montgomery, on a vagrancy
charge.[37] Sheriff Byrne apparently kept his word because he instructed the jailer that no one was to know that the prisoner was
in the jail. He also contended that he avoided discussing the circumstances of Neal's incarceration except for the fact that he
was a possible object of mob violence.[38]

Sheriff Byrne later reported that at the time he was not unduly
worried about the mob capturing Neal:

> When the Negro was brought to me I put him in what is known as the
> death cell and which is the best protected cell in the jail, and had a
> double lock put on the door. Sheriff Gandy advised me, however, that
> he would protect me and if there were any rumors of a mob being
> formed to take the Negro from my jail he would promptly notify me
> and give me the necessary assistance, but as it was not to be known
> where the prisoner was concealed I thought there was little danger
> from mob violence.[39]

Gandy made two trips from Pensacola to Brewton over the
weekend of October 20 and 21 to interrogate Neal, and on Monday, October 22, Neal confessed and implicated another Negro
from Malone, Florida, Herbert Smith; Gandy informed Sheriff
Chambliss in Marianna by phone at two o'clock that afternoon
that Neal had confessed and requested that Chambliss arrest
Smith and bring him to Pensacola to confront Neal, whose real
whereabouts was apparently kept from Chambliss.[40] Elaborate
precautions were taken by Chambliss to get the second suspect
to Pensacola. Smith was picked up at dark and taken to Tallahassee and finally routed to Pensacola by a roundabout path through

37. Pensacola *Journal*, October 26, 1934, pp. 1, 8.
38. Interview of Hugh M. Caffey with Sheriff G. S. Byrne, November, 1934, in
Miller Papers, Alabama State Archives.
39. *Ibid.*
40. Chambliss to Sholtz, October 31, 1934, in Lynching File, Series 278,
Florida State Archives.

Georgia and Alabama. Neal's confession, signed by a mark since he was illiterate, is recorded below. The authorities mistakenly spelled his name as "Neals."

Confession of Claude Neals

My name is Claude Neals. I am 23 years old and have lived at Malone, Fla., for all my life.

On Wednesday night, October 17, 1934, I spent the night with my wife and came back to Mr. Cannidy's on my wagon. My wife was with me and we went to my mother's when we left Mr. Cannidy. I had been at Mr. Cannidy's that morning helping him to break a mule to the plow. We plowed up to about twelve o'clock and then went to my mother's.

When we got to my mother's, we went out in the field to hunt a sow and I met Herbert Smith out in the field. We went up alongside of the fence to a pump on the edge of Mr. Cannidy's field. When Herbert and I got to the pump, Miss Lola Cannidy was sitting by the pump cleaning out the hog trough.

She asked me if I would clean it out and I said that I would. I sat down and washed out the trough and then pumped it full of water for Miss Lola.

When Miss Lola turned to go to the house, Herbert walked up and caught her by the arm. Herbert told her: "How about me being with you?" She said, "You must be a fool." Herbert said, "No, won't nobody know nothing about it." She told him to go ahead and go on, but Herbert pulled her by the arm and she started calling her brother, Mr. Willford. Herbert pulled her on over the fence about four or five steps away and asked me to help him put her over the fence. Herbert choked her before he asked me to help him put her over the fence and she stopped calling her brother. I helped him put her over the fence and when we got over all three of us went on down by the East and West fence to another fence running North and South and went down by the North and South fence.

When we got to the corner of the woods, about the width of 6 acres, Miss Lola said: "This is far enough." Herbert said, "Come on," and she said, "I don't want to go into the woods for snakes will bite me. I am not going any farther."

Herbert told her, "Lay down, then." She laid down with Herbert holding to her. Herbert told me to catch both of her arms and hold her and I did that. She caught my watch. Herbert pulled up Miss Lola's clothes while I held her arms and he had intercourse with her one time. She was fighting me with her hands and trying to kick Herbert off.

After he got through, Herbert said, "Come on, Claude and get yours." I told him I didn't want to do that. Then Herbert held her and I had intercourse with her.

When I got through, Herbert said: "I will fix her where she won't tell it." I told him I had been working for her brother for two years and I didn't want to do anything else to her. He said, "You are just scared as hell." I said, "Yes, I know and you do, too, what will be the consequences if this is known." Herbert said, "I'll fix her where she won't tell nobody."

Herbert then broke down a little dead oak tree and broke off a piece about 3 or 3½ feet long and hit her in the head with it. She hadn't said anything from the time we made her lie down, and she breathed a few times after Herbert hit her in the head. Herbert dragged a piece of log about five feet long and as big as my thigh up side of her and I dragged up another smaller piece and we laid them on her, or by the side of her. She just was breathing when we left her; she was not quite dead at that time.

We then left her and went back to the edge of the field down to the big hedgerow. Herbert walked down by the hedgerow and I haven't seen him since. I went to my mother's house and from there to my wife's aunt's place at Miss Rose Lewis's. I came back by Justice of the Peace Edgar Anderson's and talked to him.

I went back to my mother's and from there to Mr. John Daniel's. I was at Mr. Dave Daniels' house picking peas when the Sheriff came and got me.

This confession, made at Brewton, Alabama, on the 22nd day of October, 1934, in the presence of G. S. Byrne, Sheriff of Escambia County, Alabama, and W. E. Brooks, County Solicitor of Escambia County, Alabama, is made of my own free will and accord and without any threats, promises of reward, or hope of reward, and is entirely voluntary on my part.

(Signed) Claude X Neals[41]
mark

Why Claude Neal implicated Herbert Smith is uncertain. Reliable information suggests that he had been "whipped" by Smith in a recent fight and wished to get even.[42] Regardless, once confronted by Smith, he repudiated his original confession and admitted sole responsibility for raping and killing Lola Cannidy. Why Neal confessed is also open to question. There was no ap-

41. Confession of Claude Neals, in Miller Papers, Alabama State Archives.
42. Kester, "The Marianna, Florida Lynching," 7.

parent advantage for him in doing so. Surely, his confession, which lied about Smith's complicity, cannot be construed as an act of character. Though the wording and imagery of the confession are vivid enough to be convincing, it lacks mention of much information which was previously the basis of the case against him: the hammer thought to be the murder weapon, his bloody clothes and conversations with persons who observed the cuts on his hands. Neal may have been resigned to his death at this point either in the electric chair or at the hands of a lynch mob. It is possible that he felt this way even before his confession; this might account for his giving the confession in the first place. After Sheriff Byrne warned Neal, who had already told a fellow prisoner why he was in jail, not to disclose that type of information, Neal replied that "he did not care if they came and got him as he knew he would die in the electric chair and he would just as soon have a mob lynch him now so he could get his thoughts away from the electric chair."[43]

Events moved swiftly about Claude Neal after his confession. Byrne asked Gandy to be relieved of the responsibility for protecting Neal now that the confession had been obtained. The latter declared that "in all probability" he could return for Neal that night and place him in Fort Barrancas, a statement which implied that Gandy considered the federal jail more secure than the one at Brewton. But instead of coming for Neal that night, Gandy helped create a situation which jeopardized the prisoner's safety, perhaps because Gandy may have developed a dislike for Claude Neal. (He reputedly declared after Neal's confession that "he never wanted to kill a negro so bad in his life.") He informed the press that Neal had confessed and that he "was not in the state of Florida now, I don't think."[44]

Word on Neal's location mysteriously leaked at this point because at twelve o'clock that night the Associated Press in Mobile

43. Interview of Caffey with Byrne, November, 1934, in Miller Papers, Alabama State Archives.
44. *Ibid.;* Interview of Hugh M. Caffey with Policeman R. A. Strong of Brewton, Alabama, November, 1934, in Miller Papers, Alabama State Archives; Pensacola *Journal,* October 25, 1934, p. 3.

called Byrne and asked him to confirm a statement they had received from Florida that Neal had confessed and was in the Brewton jail. Once he recognized that his questioner was privy to intimate details of the confession, Byrne admitted Neal had confessed, but he denied that Claude Neal was still in Brewton.[45] This call was the catalyst for a quickening pace of events. A lynch caravan from Jackson County, consisting of a scout car with three or four other vehicles, began rolling northwest toward Brewton. Why was Neal's site of incarceration suddenly known after he had been successfully concealed for nearly a week? Those who had access to the ideas and actions of the group which set out to administer justice to Neal in Brewton declare that the lynchers were informed by "someone in the law enforcement agency in Pensacola who tipped off a local politician in Marianna."[46] It would seem plausible that law officers and their families were often friends who did not hesitate to supply information to one another once doubts of a suspect's solitary guilt were removed.

News of the coming of the lynch mob was forecast on Thursday afternoon, October 25, more than ten hours after Neal's second confession, when a "stranger" who represented himself as living in the lower end of town entered the sheriff's office and began a conversation with two residents of Brewton, one a justice of the peace, about the Claude Neal case. One of the persons in the office recalled:

> He told us that a mob of 300 to 400 people had formed in Florida for the Negro, and that he thought that they had found out he was in the Brewton jail; that he understood that they had found it out through the Negro, Herbert Smith, who had been brought here after Claude Neals [sic] implicated him in the affair and was thereafter released in Florida. He further said that he thought the sheriff here had received

45. Interview of Caffey with Byrne, November, 1934, in Miller Papers, Alabama State Archives.
46. Author's interviews with Mr. A., December 28, 1977, and Mr. B., December 29, 1977. Mr. A. was a close friend of a member of the lynch mob who described the entire expedition to him before he died. Mr. B. is a prominent citizen of Jackson County who has pieced together information on the mob's activities through contacts with several members of the group. Because of the nature of this material, it must obviously remain confidential.

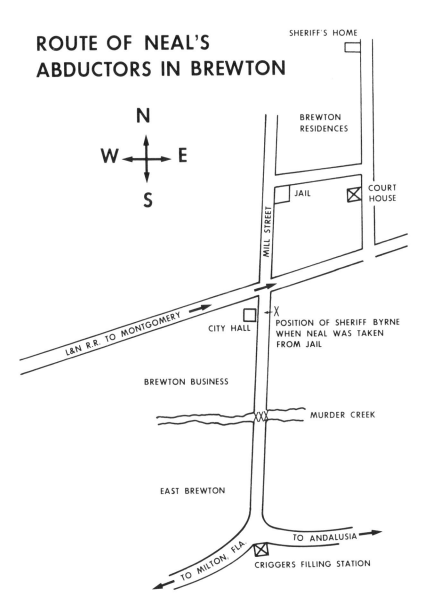

Fig. 5. Route of Neal's abductors in Brewton.
Map by Jerome F. Coling

orders to send him to Pensacola. . . . When we expressed surprise he
said he thought we already knew it or he would not have told us, and
nothing more was particularly said on the subject.[47]

The visitor had displayed remarkable knowledge of the intri-
cacies of the situation since Herbert Smith was still in the Escambia County jail in Florida. His key statement probably came
near the end of his conversation when he queried declaratively
that "he thought" the sheriff had received orders to send Neal to
Pensacola.

By late afternoon on Friday, one week after Lola Cannidy's body
had been discovered, a group in Jackson County began organizing
for a run on the Brewton jail. They planned to arrive when the
town would be asleep and police protection minimal. By going in
only a few cars they hoped to avoid suspicion before and after
they seized Neal. They decided to use only late model automobiles for the round trip of approximately three hundred miles so
they might race cross-country if necessary. Though the raiding
party was small, its members were experienced in the use of
weapons as well as with explosives. By prearrangement they met
quietly after nightfall and set out together toward Brewton on
Alabama roads.

They arrived there after midnight. T. J. Criggers, operator of the
Gulf gas station at the end of the pavement in East Brewton, provided the following description to a court solicitor:

> Three cars stopped at my filling station on the night of October 25th,
> around 1:45 o'clock in the morning. I am positive two of the cars bore
> Florida tags, but not certain as to the third one. I would not be exact
> but there was around five people to the car. I know five men were in
> each of the two cars that I gassed. I am not familiar with so many
> people around here, as I am a native of Texas. I resided in Flomaton
> six months prior to the time I came to Brewton and have only been
> here about one month. It might be possible that I could identify some
> of the occupants of the cars that stopped at my station, and I am in-
> clined to believe that I could. They were just the ordinary run of
> people, with no particular distinguishing marks. The driver was well
> dressed in a blue suit; three of them had on overalls.

47. Interview of Hugh M. Caffey with Lum Jeter, November, 1934, in Miller
Papers, Alabama State Archives.

Some member of this crowd asked who the Sheriff was and I told them. They asked what county this was and I told them, and then they wanted to know how far it was to the Florida line, and I told them it was around 8 miles to Jay, Florida, and pointed out the Milton road that runs by my place.

These cars came into my place of business from the direction of Andalusia [Alabama], and not on the Milton road, my filling station being in the forks of these roads.

I did not see any cars come back by, for after selling them gas at that time of night, I went on back to bed.[48]

The Brewton police first heard about the mystery cars from Dan Brantley, who came into town about 1:45 A.M. to pick up his daughter who was employed at the local silk mill. Brantley had heard that afternoon from one of the men who had talked with the stranger at the courthouse that "the Negro" was in the Brewton jail and that a mob was coming after him, and so he reported to the policemen on duty: "In passing through East Brewton and at the end of the pavement there, I noticed three automobiles which were obtaining gas at the Gulf Station. . . . There were at least fifteen people standing and walking around." He added that he believed this crowd was "in to lynch the Negro." While two local police officers on duty had seen the cars with Florida tags traveling about Brewton before Brantley contacted them, they did not suspect a lynching party.[49] When one of the cars stopped in front of the courthouse a person inside the car told a policeman who had pulled up his car behind them that his associates were Florida police officers and that they wanted to see the sheriff. Upon hearing that the sheriff was at home, they asked whether the jail was located on top of the courthouse. The policeman declared it was not and told them where it was located. At this point the drivers of the Florida cars turned around and drove in the direction of the Gulf station to fill up for their return trip. When Brantley later alerted the police with his suspicions, they called the jailer, Jake Shanholtzer, and warned him to "look out"

48. Interview of Hugh M. Caffey with T. V. Criggers, November, 1934, in Miller Papers, Alabama State Archives.
49. Interviews of Hugh M. Caffey with Dan Brantley and R. A. Strong, November 1934, in Miller Papers, Alabama State Archives.

because Dan Brantley had said there were about three hundred people in the mob. Shanholtzer, who must have felt very lonely at this time, sounded the alarm for Sheriff Byrne and his deputy, who arrived within minutes.[50] The sheriff described the action of the next few minutes.

> When I got to the jail there were two or three cars there and two of the men got out of one of the cars and talked to me and one got out holding an automatic shot gun on me. They demanded the Negro of me and I gave them the assurance that he was not in the jail, but had been carried away. I attempted to placate them by assuring them that if he was in my jail I would be glad to turn him over to them, and went so far as to offer carrying them through the jail and letting them see for themselves, feeling that I had safely concealed the Negro in the death cell, and that after looking over the Negro prisoners in the regular cells they would leave satisfied. They expressed confidence that I had told them the truth, shook hands with me and left. As soon as they left I got in my car to trail them to determine if they were leaving by way of Pensacola or by way of Milton, for if they were taking the Milton road I was coming back and take him to Evergreen. I trailed the cars on the Milton road until I reached the bridge across Murder Creek which divides Brewton from East Brewton and as I saw them continue in that direction I turned around and came back towards the jail. I stopped in front of the City Hall where policemen R. A. Strong and Cates were standing and told them I might need their assistance a little later.[51]

As later evidence would establish, the sheriff had been decoyed out of position. The first group which appeared at the jail had withdrawn, probably intending to confuse the police and lull them into complacency. While Byrne was pursuing them at a safe distance, the real assault, probably from the cluster of three cars that had been noted at the Gulf station and in other places in the community, was launched on the frightened jailer who, only minutes before, had been comforted by the deputy that Sheriff Byrne had outsmarted the lynchers. Just as the deputy's car turned the corner following the sheriff, the three Florida cars

50. Interview of Hugh M. Caffey with Jake Shanholtzer, November, 1934, in Miller Papers, Alabama State Archives.
51. Interview of Caffey with Byrne, November, 1934, in Miller Papers, Alabama State Archives.

drove up and their occupants rushed the jail and demanded the keys to look through the "Negro cells." The jailer recalled:

> One of the men was behind the ones that held guns on me and had an arm full of dynamite. He said that he would blow the place off the corner if they did not find what they were looking for. They took the keys from me and being unable to unlock the cell, held their guns on a white trusty in jail and compelled him to unlock the doors. They might have overlooked the Negro in the death cell if he had not rushed to the door to see what it was all about, but as soon as they saw him they expressed satisfaction, had the cell unlocked and took him away.[52]

The jailer said that the leaders tied Neal's hands with a plow rope and placed him in the backseat of a waiting automobile. Apparently, the conspirators were well schooled in procedures to outwit the law because they said very little to one another while they removed Neal. The jailer overheard one of them remark to Neal, however, that "if he had any talking to do to the Lord he had better do it now because he didn't have long to live."[53] And just before the group left one of the leaders told the jailer that "they were not going to kill the Negro themselves but were going to take him back to the father of the girl whom he had attacked and let him do it."[54]

This contingent, with Neal in the backseat of the first car between two white men, sped in the direction of East Brewton past Sheriff Byrne and two policemen talking in front of the courthouse. Instead of giving chase, Byrne chose to return to the jail and discovered that his prisoner had been taken. He immediately telephoned Sheriff Gandy.

Descriptions of the dress of the group together with the skill with which they executed the seizure and escape suggest that they were more knowledgeable than the average Jackson County farmer. The Gulf station attendant noted that the driver of one car was "well dressed in a blue suit." Sheriff Byrne later identified

52. Interview of Caffey with Shanholtzer, November, 1934, in Miller Papers, Alabama State Archives.
53. Brewton *Standard*, November 1, 1934, pp. 1, 8.
54. Interview of Caffey with Shanholtzer, November, 1934, in Miller Papers, Alabama State Archives.

the clothing of three of the men: "The two to whom I talked were well dressed in dark clothes and the one man who held the automatic on me was dressed in khaki clothes."[55] A policeman who saw best the man who stopped his car and claimed to be a Florida officer described him as wearing khaki pants, a flannel shirt, and boots. Apparently, he was dressed in the garb of a Florida officer of that time because the policeman saw no reason to question his claim. Neal's capture had been accomplished with finesse. It required knowledge of police operations as well as expert planning. Although lynch mobs frequently intimidate police because they outnumber them, this group relied largely on its wits. They exploited the fact that Florida police officers had been traveling to Brewton to investigate Neal, and they located the sheriff and the jail without directing suspicion to themselves. When Byrne did appear, they apparently had an alternate plan to draw him away from the jail, a critical move because he was the one person who might have felt sufficient responsibility for Neal to try to defend him. They also accomplished this mission without awakening the townspeople. As the Brewton *Standard* noted in its next edition: "So quietly did the mob do its work here that no one except the officers who encountered them knew anything about what was going on until the next morning. Residents living within less than 100 yards of the jail were undisturbed in their sleep by the occurrence, and there was no excitement attendant upon its entry to and exit from the city."[56]

The abductors reassured one another on their way back to Jackson County that Neal was "so low" he didn't deserve a trial. They had taken illegal actions which would lead to the lynching of Claude Neal because they felt justified to do so. While murder is usually a personal deed, lynching, in the sense of the execution of another person by a self-constituted group with accompanying public rituals, is a social act; it requires confidence in community approval.

55. Interviews of Caffey with Strong and Byrne, November, 1934, in Miller Papers, Alabama State Archives.
56. Brewton *Standard*, October 25, 1934, p. 1.

Chapter 4

Vengeance for Justice

The effective execution of their mission to abduct Neal and return him to Jackson County underlined the backgrounds and abilities of the men who comprised the lynch mob. Occupationally, they were not at the top of the status or income scales—not the merchants, furnishing men, or progressive politicians seeking to build the reputation of their city and county as a good place for investments and population growth. That group wished to avoid identification with lynch law at all costs. The band that seized Neal might be defined as middle to lower-middle class: clerks, salesmen, mechanics, petty merchants, servicers, and farmers. Their status accounts for the fact that several of them were identified as "well dressed," an observation which probably surprised Brewton policemen because they did not expect lynchers to be so attired. They were early middle-aged (probably only one was in his twenties) and enjoyed a good reputation in their communities as reasonable, church-going men who had a marked sense of civic responsibility. Although they probably all knew one another before their expedition to the Brewton jail, they came from several different communities in Jackson County, principally Malone, Greenwood, and Marianna. The nucleus of the group derived from family ties, especially from kinsmen of a local politician, and personal friendships. Key members learned of Neal's location very soon after it was divulged, and they exercised personal skills in police detection in finding the victim. For those who were army veterans, the raid seemed to revive the spirit of the Great Crusade, seventeen years after America had gone to war.

Since members of the mob were "in-between" people, they were economically solvent even during the Depression; they had money, good cars, and sufficient free time from their jobs to permit them to make a two-day commitment to lynch Neal. They were also comfortable enough to focus their attention exclusively on the moral rather than economic implications of social problems, and hence the rape question. But they had seldom had a hand in great enterprises. They knew their betters in the community, though in this instance the elite business leaders and professional persons would not provide leadership. The situation was made to order for those who sought to inflate their self-esteem by seeking a larger leadership role. Whether they were also seeking public acclaim is uncertain; the group remained quiet about its identity, although the national attention which the Neal incident provoked may have accounted for their reticence.[1]

The lynchers probably returned to Jackson County while it was still dark. They apparently avoided major highways on their trip. The owner of the Gulf station in Brewton testified that instead of returning directly on Florida Highway 90, the best thoroughfare, they drove toward Andalusia, Alabama. Evidence suggests that they traveled along back roads in Alabama until they had nearly reached their destination at a point on the Chattahoochee River. By following this course they avoided possible confrontation with sheriffs and deputies in Jackson and adjacent counties who might have been alerted had they used Florida roads. Their trip was completed about six o'clock in the morning; they encamped in the deep woods to plan the lynching of Neal on Friday night,

---

1. Most of this information comes from Mr. A., a reputable citizen of Marianna who was active in community affairs in the 1930s. At least five other prominent figures in the white community of Marianna contributed corroborating material. All this information is confidential. A member of the lynch mob confessed details about the mob's membership and activities, and about Neal's response before his death. These interviews took place between September 26 and December 29, 1977.

October 26. Their precautions were unnecessary because Sheriff Gandy of Escambia County, Florida, did not inform Sheriff Chambliss of Jackson County of the jailbreak in Brewton until 8:00 A.M., six hours after the fact and after the Brewton sheriff had notified Gandy. Chambliss was probably reporting honestly when he wrote in his chronicle that at 9:00 A.M. that day, "Ways and means of saving Neal from mob discussed and considered, but whereabouts and destination of the mob uncertain."[2] Although Chambliss would be severely censured by Brewton newspapers for asserting that afternoon that Neal might have already been lynched in Alabama, his statement was consistent with the fact that Neal's abductors had taken him across south Alabama and had apparently kept him there for several hours. Their choice of travel over roads in Alabama also gives greater credibility to Chambliss' later defense of what seemed his ineffectual handling of the situation: "I tried to surround Jackson County with deputies, but we never did see the mob."[3]

That Friday, Chambliss was actually more concerned about the fact that a pair of bank robbers had shot and killed one of his two deputies. The robbers' fate grimly interfaced with the lynching of Claude Neal and its aftermath. Buford Mears and Miles Dudley, both whites, were tried and convicted of robbing a bank in Malone, Florida, in Jackson County Court while Neal was sequestered in Brewton. Although both men were young, they had had several altercations with the law and had been jailed on violations of prohibition. After being apprehended in Chicago for their robbery, they were returned to Marianna and given twenty-year sentences for their crimes. While they were in court, someone slipped a gun to Mears. As Chambliss and his deputy were transporting Mears and Dudley, handcuffed together in the backseat, to the Chipley jail Thursday night, October 25, Mears called upon the officers to halt the car and instantly fired into the back

2. Interview of Hugh M. Caffey with T. V. Criggers, November, 1934, in Governor B. M. Miller Papers, Alabama State Archives, Montgomery; Sheriff W. Flake Chambliss to Governor David Sholtz, October 31, 1934, in Lynching File, Series 278, Florida State Archives, Tallahassee.

3. Author's interviews with Mr. A., December 15, 1977, and Mr. B., December 16, 1977; Tallahassee *Democrat*, November 1, 1934, p. 8.

of the deputy in the front seat. Sheriff Chambliss, a hulking but agile man, released the wheel of the car and dived for Mears's gun while the deputy, who later died from his wounds, was able to shoot and mortally wound a third prisoner. Though the car careened out of control and landed in an embankment, Chambliss was able to regain custody of the prisoners.[4]

The drama involving the young criminals provided a backdrop for the Neal affair. Undoubtedly, it quickened fears in the local population that lawlessness was getting the upper hand and that forceful action was required to restore order. There were threats of mob action against Mears, a surviving bank robber. But he was taken briefly to Panama City to assure his safety, and National Guardsmen accompanied him in all his subsequent courtroom appearances. The standard judicial processes accorded the desperado, despite the scope and verifiability of his crimes, would contrast sharply with the vigilante action taken against Neal.

The different justice assigned to the two men dramatized the greater anger against Neal and the more intense desire to punish him. Although the fury of the population had been balked when the mob searched nearly every jail in northwest Florida and was unable to find him, Neal was still the main topic of angry conversation in the county; each day that passed without news of his location stirred residents to greater impatience. There were rumors that a local Ku Klux Klan might be reorganized and that it would issue a challenge to the civil government to recover Neal or the Klan would do so. On October 23, three days before Neal was returned to Marianna, more than a thousand subscribers to the *Daily Times-Courier* read a front-page heading: "Ku Klux Klan May Ride Again, Jackson County Citizens May Rally to Fiery Cross to Protect Womanhood." The article reported:

> Taking a determined stand to protect the honor of womanhood and to champion the oppressed in Jackson County, a group of sober-minded, straight forward men will probably organize a local Ku Klux

4. Chambliss to Sholtz, October 31, 1934, in Lynching File, Series 278, Florida State Archives; Jackson County *Floridan*, October 26, 1934, p. 1.

Klan, it was revealed to the writer the other day by a prominent . . .
citizen.

The purpose of the Klan is to take over where the law fails, or where
the law has no jurisdiction. It will defend and protect the constitution
and the flag of the United States and make this section safe for "life,
liberty and the pursuit of happiness."[5]

Blacks in Jackson County were quick to perceive the climate
of terror developing over the Cannidy murder and tried desper-
ately to placate whites for fear that the entire Negro population
would suffer from implication with Neal. Local blacks wrote letters to each of the newspapers in Marianna, declaring their hope
that those guilty would be caught and the innocent spared from
retribution. Eight black citizens, including the principal of the
local high school for blacks, wrote the editor of the *Floridan*
while Neal was still in Brewton.

> Allow us to say through the columns of your widely read paper that
> we, the colored citizens of Jackson County, Florida, do here and now,
> stamp our disapproval upon the brutal murder of one of our white
> citizens last Thursday near Greenwood, Fla. The family have our
> deepest sympathy, and the law our unstinted support, in bringing the
> guilty to speedy justice.
>
> We do not condone crime in any form. We believe in, and teach our
> Race to be law-abiding citizens. We trust that the brutal act supposed
> to have been committed by one of our Race will not break that
> friendly and mutual relationship that exists among the white and col-
> ored citizens of Jackson County, one of the best counties in the State.
> We have the uttermost confidence in the best white citizens of the
> county, and trust you have the same in us. We shall ever strive and
> teach our Race to never betray that trust. We pray that you will get
> the guilty brutes and protect the innocent.[6]

The letter was signed "Your humble citizens."

Another black man, John Curry, who was even more frightened, wrote the *Daily Times-Courier* on October 22. He was virtually prepared to concede that Neal was responsible for the

---

5. Marianna *Daily Times-Courier*, October 23, 1934, p. 1.
6. Howard A. Kester, "The Marianna, Florida Lynching," 10, in Lynching File,
Series 278, Florida State Archives.

crime in exchange for the return of a peaceable state to the community. Curry wrote:

> To the White Citizens of Jackson County:
>
> Just a few lines to let you all know that we good colored citizens of Jackson County don't feel no sympathy toward the nigger that———— the white lady and killed her. No! We haven't felt he did right because he should stay in his place, and since he did such as he did, we are not feeling that we have a right to plead to you all for mercy.
>
> It makes us chagrined and feel that he has ruined the good colored people that try to behave themselves and work for an honest living.
>
> I feel very bad over it myself to see that we have such a fellow in the Race and I am among the good colored people that feel just like I do toward him. I talked with them, and they can't see how they can have sympathy for him.
>
> But I am writing to let you know that we leave it to you all to do what you all see fit to do to him. But still asking you all not to be hard on your good servants that have been honest and faithful for the time that we have been working with you for the other fellow. Because we good colored people want to thank you all for the favors and the chance that you will have given us to let us have schools for our children and teachers to teach them and jobs for us to work and to get bread for them that they can have a chance. Also we thank you all for making it easy.
>
> Because if it wasn't for the good white citizens, we realize that many of our girls and boys would have been mobbed for nothing they done but for the brutal act that was done. I also thank the sheriff for working so faithfully to get the right man.
>
> Your faithful servant,
John Curry
>
> still pleading for a chance for the better class of colored people and not to punish us for him, because if he do wrong he is wrong, and we have no sympathy for him![7]

The lynch mob was exhilarated by the same climate of opinion which frightened the area's blacks. The whites of the mob demonstrated confidence throughout that their actions would be approved or at least not be opposed by residents and officials in northwest Florida. They were not deterred by the local editor who had courageously appealed earlier for the law to take its

7. *Ibid.*, 9.

course.[8] Apparently they saw themselves as defenders of a
"higher law" and did not encounter opposition which forced a
reassessment of the morality or legality of their actions. The information which leaked from Pensacola on Neal's location was
merely one sign of social approval, and the sympathetic response
of law officers toward members of the lynch mob was another. It
is significant that even in Brewton, where at least token resistance was offered, not a single person among the five who made
contact with the lynch party would be able to identify its members again. The vigilantes had a sense of attacking an empty for-
tress; their problem was merely to locate the hiding place. Except
for Sheriff Chambliss, who took unusual risks in denying information on Neal's location after the murder of Lola Cannidy, the
general message conveyed by law enforcement officials was that
the life of a black man was not worth risking the lives of the
police. Members of the mob could therefore be nonchalant about
their intention to murder. They apparently were unconcerned
about transporting Neal across a state line, a deed conceivably
punishable by death under the Lindbergh Act. They also made no
effort to conceal their faces or their license plates.[9]

Sheriff Byrne of Escambia County was mistaken when, during
a news conference the morning after the prisoner's seizure, he
stated to newsmen that Neal had probably already been lynched.
Rather Neal was bound and kept under close guard in a woodland
area several miles from the Cannidy farm. A few of the vigilantes
probably left the compound to purchase food and liquor, others
to inform the Cannidy family that Neal would be turned over to
them that evening and that "women in the family would be
given the first chance with him, then the men." A crowd of sight-
seers as well as friends and neighbors began to assemble Friday
afternoon, October 26, at the Cannidy home; there they were
met with handshakes and welcomes from members of the bereaved family. George Cannidy, the father, sometimes greeted

8. Jackson County *Floridan*, October 26, 1934, p. 2.
9. No observers of the lynch mob in Panama City, Chipley, or Brewton reported
them as wearing masks or concealing their license plates.

visitors by patting a large revolver stuck in his belt and telling them what he intended to do when he got his hands on "the nigger."[10] Members of the mob even felt sufficiently justified in their intent to lynch Claude Neal to make their determination known through public media.

The Friday afternoon edition of the *Eagle*, published in Dothan, Alabama, a short distance from Marianna, stated in headlines, "Florida to Burn Negro at Stake: Sex Criminal Seized from Brewton Jail, Will be Mutilated, Set Afire in Extra-Legal Vengeance for Deed," and the Dothan radio station announced the impending event several times. The mob, or those privy to its secrets, even called the sheriff of adjacent Washington County in Florida and notified him of the time for the scheduled lynching. They also spread word that the place would be the Cannidy property. And in the words of a reporter for the *Eagle*, "For hours as word of the jail storming and seizure spread, the grapevines and telephones of Northwest Florida buzzed and grim faced farmers prepared to make the Cannidy home their rendezvous." The reporter declared, "They knew what was to happen: that was freely bruited and the Negro bound securely at the stake waited. The mobsmen and the citizens of Northwest Florida waited for nightfall when the Negro is destined to pay the extra-legal penalty for his crimes—the murder and outraging of the white girl. . . . The Negro is to be carried to the spot where he committed the crime a week ago."[11]

It is doubtful if the abductors of Neal also informed the Associated Press about their "invitational lynching." Apparently they overestimated their ability to confine this type of sensational information, upon disclosure, to their own immediate area. By 3:00 P.M., however, AP was disseminating data about the lynching on its national circuit. One of its correspondents was apparently so confounded by the news that he made a special point to contact Walter White, executive secretary of the National Association for

10. Dothan *Eagle*, October 26, 1934, pp. 1, 6.
11. *Ibid.*

the Advancement of Colored People.[12] White's telegram to Florida Governor David Sholtz, asking his intervention, could hardly have been anticipated by the group that held Neal because their actions appeared to be based on assumptions of sovereign territoriality.

The telegrams from White and others produced their desired effect.[13] Since Florida law specified, however, that the governor could send the National Guard only upon request of a county sheriff, Sholtz could go no further, short of declaring martial law, than to inform Sheriff Chambliss that he had authorized the use of the Guard in Marianna. Chambliss replied negatively to the proposal, declaring that he thought he was able to handle any situation which might arise. He informed the governor about several places where the lynching might take place and that he had sworn in a force of thirty-two deputies and a dozen special officers to stop the vigilantes. Those who knew Chambliss do not ascribe his decision to personal confidence. One friend recalls him shaking his head despairingly and saying, "All Hell is going to break loose around here." Another, a regular poker-playing companion, described him as "the most worried man you ever saw." It is doubtful that Sheriff Chambliss could have prevented the lynching. One deputy sheriff implied as much when he told a local reporter during the afternoon of October 26, "In my opinion, the mob will not be bothered, either before or after the lynching."[14]

Whatever the personal intentions of Sheriff Chambliss, who was a generous and considerate man and fearless when administering the law to the likes of bank robbers, he felt ineffective in

12. Walter White to Governor David Sholtz, October 26, 1934, in Lynching File, Series 278, Florida State Archives.
13. Copies of these telegrams are in the Official Correspondence of Governor David Sholtz, Florida State Archives.
14. J. P. Newell (Governor Sholtz's Executive Secretary) to Mrs. Walter S. Jones, November 1, 1934, in Sholtz Correspondence, Florida State Archives; Montgomery *Advertiser*, October 27, 1934, p. 1; Author's interviews with Filmore Sims, September 27, 1977, and with Mr. A., December 15, 1977; Marianna *Daily Times-Courier*, October 27, 1934, p. 1.

the face of the lynch mob. Despite the fact that several hundred cars stopped in the vicinity of the Cannidy home that night, no lawmen were observed in the crowd. Chambliss tried later to explain his performance by declaring that he and his deputies were looking for the lynchers, not the larger crowd which had assembled to watch the summary punishment.[15]

While the lynch mob waited for darkness, Neal was not tortured or subjected to indignities, although he was again asked whether he wished to repent. He refused to do so and maintained an outward calm. Curiously, he continued to use the deferential formalities of address which blacks employed in conversations with whites, including "sir" and "kind gentlemen."[16]

Nightfall lent a bacchanalian quality to the scene at the Cannidy farm. Bonfires were lit in several places. These illuminated numerous sharp-pointed sticks in neat bundles close by. They also disclosed the ruddy faces and farm dress of the men, women, and children who wouldn't have missed an opportunity like this for anything. They talked loudly and drank a lot and some yelled that they wanted a piece of Neal's body as a souvenir. Men wore guns in plain view. Everyone there had already agreed with approving eyes that it would be all right to shoot at the corpse once the family had had its way. Before long the members of the crowd became more animated and more friendly with one another as if they had made a pact. As each car drove up the sandy roads to the Cannidy homestead, the crowd waited breathlessly for its lights to pass through the churning dust and the long line of parked cars on either side of the road. If a motorist mistakenly drove past the cars because he hoped to find a more convenient parking place, some persons would dash over and peer in the windows and register disgust over their disappointment that it was not the men bringing Neal. The crowd was ready to lynch; indeed, the group which held Neal began to fear that it had become uncontrollable and that its members might injure one another. One eyewitness

---

15. Pensacola *Journal*, October 27, 1934, p. 1; Tallahassee *Democrat*, October 27, 1934, p. 1, November 1, 1934, pp. 1, 8.

16. Author's interview with Mr. A., December 15, 1977.

remembers, "The whole county up there was backed up with people."[17]

There are various estimates of the number of spectators. A reporter for a Marianna newspaper observed "hundreds of cars, carrying a crowd estimated at between three and five thousand people including women and children and representing eleven states." A Dothan newsman who witnessed the evening's events described the crowd's growth during the day and evening: "Word spread like wildfire over the farming section of Jackson County and so as night drew close there were hundreds of persons at the Cannidy house." Numerous cars came to Greenwood that afternoon with drivers asking directions of filling station attendants to the site of the impending lynching. A delegation of American Legionnaires from Nebraska, en route to a convention in Miami, stopped for three hours in Marianna to see if the lynching would actually take place. According to a reporter who was present, "By seven o'clock between one thousand and two thousand persons had gathered. In another half hour the assembly had swelled to more than two thousand. Automobiles were parked on both sides of the road from the Cannidy home for more than a mile." C. L. Watford, who owned the only telephone in Greenwood, went to the Cannidy farm as late as ten o'clock and reported to the Associated Press that there was still a crowd of more than a thousand persons at the scene.[18]

Leaders in the crowd tried vainly to quiet the group about 7 P.M. so that the event could be started. Though the crowd was described by an AP correspondent then on the scene as "good natured," the leaders kept asking it to be "orderly when they bring the nigger over here." The crowd shouted, "We will!" and promised "to give the family the first chance" once he was deliv-

17. Montgomery *Advertiser*, October 27, 1934, p. 1; Author's interview with Mr. B., who participated in the crowd as observer, December 16, 1977; Interview of Walter Howard with Mr. B., August 15, 1977.

18. Jackson County *Floridan*, November 2, 1934, p. 1; Dothan *Eagle*, October 27, 1934, pp. 1, 5; Author's interview with Nick Pender, December 15, 1977; Pensacola *Journal*, October 27, 1934, p. 1; Chicago *Daily Tribune*, October 27, 1934, p. 1.

ered. At 7:30 the leaders were apparently still confident that they could lynch Neal in the promised place. They lined up cars in front of the Cannidy house to form a barricade between the crowd and the Cannidy family and ordered everyone "to stand back and give the family plenty of room." The family, some of them armed, stood in the middle of a semicircle of eager viewers. At this point, the leaders announced again that the womenfolks would do what they wanted to "the nigger," then the men would get him. To this proposal, the crowd responded its enthusiastic approval with "All right!" The spokesman for the lynching party then ordered the crowd to become quiet or "the nigger" would not be delivered. And when the enthusiastic talk and raucous laughter subsided, one leader announced, "They're going to bring him in." The crowd became silent. Yet the promise was not fulfilled, and the assembly soon burst forth again in loud talk. Several more promises were made contingent on the crowd's orderliness, but Neal did not appear in the semicircle. Each time it became more difficult to obtain the response the leaders sought, and the crowd became more and more restless. An AP correspondent reported that "a man who identified himself as a member of the Florida legislature made a humorous address and promised action but urged his audience to be quiet." But to no avail. The crowd's excitement, teased by the leaders and inflamed by drinking Jackson County moonshine whiskey, had reached feverish proportions. Although the "committee," as the leaders came to be identified, later declared that they had been fearful to produce Neal because "the nigger was so low down they didn't want anyone to get hurt on his account,"[19] it seems more likely that they were afraid that they might be held criminally responsible for injuries or deaths suffered by whites in the turbulent crowd.

The committee made one more desperate attempt to fulfill its promise to the Cannidy family. About nine o'clock they tried to slip the family through the throng to the scene where Miss Cannidy was murdered. George Cannidy, who still believed that he

19. Montgomery *Advertiser*, October 28, 1934, p. 1; Dothan *Eagle*, October 27, 1934, p. 5; Boston *Herald*, October 27, 1934, p. 1; Author's interview with M. D. Cannidy, December 29, 1977.

would be given the opportunity to kill Neal personally, preferred that place because he feared that he would be "haunted" if he killed Neal in his front yard. When someone alerted the group standing in the semicircle to the fact that the family had been removed to a spot across the road about a quarter of a mile from the house, the crowd, sensing that something was going to happen at last, dashed enthusiastically to get new positions. They formed a circle around the family and lit nearly a dozen fires. The crowd became quiet again. Leaders yelled out instructions that everyone had to follow the orders of the committee and proceeded to remove troublemakers from the inner circle surrounding the family. When Neal was still not produced, rumors spread among the crowd that he had already been killed or had been taken to a state prison nearby. The onlookers finally became so frustrated that they broke ranks, left the circle and began to shout derisive remarks at the leaders. Pleas to "get back" went unheeded, and some of the crowd began to demand in unison, "We want the nigger!" All further reminders that they couldn't have him until they observed orders produced only volleys of sarcastic remarks. Some even cursed those in charge and taunted, "You ain't even got the nigger." The leaders apparently promised in response that they would see to it that Neal's body was hung in the courthouse square for everybody to see. By ten o'clock many in the crowd had gone home. Others remained, however, sensing that something was still going to happen. As the night became chilly they gathered firewood and prepared for a long wait.[20]

The committee also retired from the scene and sent word to the group of men who held Neal on the Chattahoochee River that it would not be safe to bring him to the Cannidy's farm. Whether the committee was part of the group which had wrested Neal from Brewton or simply served as a liaison with that group is uncertain. It seems likely that several of the original group also comprised the committee. Regardless, whether they had seized Neal or were merely accomplices, they demonstrated confidence

20. Dothan *Eagle*, October 27, 1934, p. 5.

that the community approved their actions by showing their faces brazenly before thousands of people.

The Cannidy family, who profess to this day that family members did not know who abducted Neal or later lynched him, understood simply that their benefactors would "take care of everything" and see to it that Neal was delivered. Neal's captors were forced, now, however, into a new and unexpected role—that of killing him. It is doubtful if everyone in the group wished to do so. The torture to which Neal was subjected from 10 P.M. to 12 P.M. that night disturbed some members of the group; one man threw up at the sight. But the most aggressive took charge. They may have been assisted by jugs of Jackson County moonshine whiskey. One man who "accompanied the mob," which wanted to use his 1930 Ford, stated, "A lot of the boys wanted to get their hands on him so bad they could hardly stand it." He recalls that in their first efforts to lynch Neal, the limb broke under his weight and they were forced "to string him up again."[21]

Howard Kester, the NAACP investigator, learned the morbid details of the lynching ten days after it occurred when he talked for one hour and forty minutes with a member of the mob. Kester, who declared that he was "quite nauseated by the things which apparently gave this man the greatest delight to relate," described the man's revelations, "corroborated by others," as follows:

> "After taking the nigger to the woods about four miles from Greenwood, they cut off his penis. He was made to eat it. Then they cut off his testicles and made him eat them and say he liked it." (I gathered that this barbarous act consumed considerable time and that other means of torture were used from time to time on Neal). "Then they sliced his sides and stomach with knives and every now and then somebody would cut off a finger or toe. Red hot irons were used on the nigger to burn him from top to bottom." From time to time during the torture a rope would be tied around Neal's neck and he was pulled up over a limb and held there until he almost choked to death when he would be let down and the torture begin all over again.[22]

21. Interview of author and Walter Howard with M. D. Cannidy family, December 30, 1977; Author's interview with Mr. A., December 27, 1977; Interview of Walter Howard with Mr. B., August 17, 1977.

22. Kester, "The Marianna, Florida Lynching," 3.

The man who castrated Neal seemed ecstatic over his handi-work. Castration of animals was a common practice in farm com-munities at the time, and some members of the group had the required skill to commit this act.

Neal must have confounded the group by his composure in the process. After suffering torture, he asked them, "Kind sirs, do one of you have a cigarette?" He died without remorse or protest, accepting his fate as a Negro who was in bad trouble with white folks, as he had from the beginning.[23]

Although the lynch mob had vented its rage on the offender, their vengeance had been unleashed in a private sanctuary in the dense woods. The thousands who had gathered earlier to partici-pate had yet to exorcise their anger. Those unable to attack Neal while alive or to witness his destruction wished to commit an act of aggression against his corpse and, after he was interred, against others of his race. The lynch mob delivered Neal's body shortly after 1 A.M. to the Cannidy house; and the crowd rushed up to see him and someone called, "There he is sure as the world." A reporter who was present described the scene: "In a few minutes several cars, one after the other, rolled into the yard. From one of them a rope jerked spasmodically as the car struck bumps and gullies [in the road]. On the end of the rope was Neal dead. His body was covered with dust, scarred and torn by knives and horribly mutilated."

When the car dragging Neal's body arrived in front of the Can-nidy house, the man riding the rear bumper cut the rope. The lynch mob having completed its task literally cut itself away from the incident at that point. Its members did not participate in later actions against blacks. They were last seen talking quietly to the Cannidy family and then driving off. The Cannidy family now assembled in front of the house with a remnant of the larger crowd which had gathered earlier in the evening. Sev-eral people drove knives into the corpse, reportedly "tearing the body almost to shreds." Sixty-year-old George Cannidy then took a .45 and pumped three bullets into the forehead of the corpse,

23. Author's interview with several persons privy to the actions of the mob, September 17, 1977; Author's interview with Mr. A., December 27, 1977.

intended as retaliation for the damage Neal inflicted on his daughter. He cried out, "They done me wrong!" complaining bitterly that the lynchers had not fulfilled their promise to give him the first crack at Neal.[24]

The crowd then had its way. Howard Kester's informants told him that many people subjected the body to other indignities. Several kicked it and others drove cars over it. Perhaps the most terrifying remark in Kester's summary of the Neal lynching was this one:

> It is reported from reliable sources that the little children, some of them mere tots, who lived in the Greenwood neighborhood, waited with sharpened sticks for the return of Neal's body and that when it rolled in the dust on the road that awful night these little children drove their weapons deep into the flesh of the dead man.[25]

As a final retribution for the outrages supposedly committed by Neal and other blacks, especially his mother and aunt, the crowd then rushed to the slope and burned every shack owned by blacks.[26]

The residents of Marianna read in a special edition of the *Daily Times-Courier* on Saturday morning, October 27, the headlines, "Girl Slayer Lynched This A.M." and "Nude Body, Terribly Mutilated, Hanging from Tree on Court House Lawn Since 3 O'Clock This Morning." Ensuing columns stated:

> Claude Neal, Greenwood Negro, was lynched last night ... somewhere in the county by a well organized orderly mob which had waited patiently for hours to avenge the death of pretty Lola Cannidy. After slashing and shooting him into mincemeat the mob took the Negro to the home of George Cannidy ... and dumped the body in the front yard. From there another mob was organized and it brought his body to the courthouse at 3 o'clock this morning where it hanged him on a tree on the east side of the courthouse lawn. His nude body was hanging at that place at an early hour this morning. After stringing him up in the tree the mob quickly dispersed.[27]

24. Dothan *Eagle*, October 27, 1934, pp. 1, 5; Author's interview with Mr. A., December 15, 1977.
25. Kester, "The Marianna, Florida Lynching," 4.
26. Author's interview with M. D. Cannidy, December 30, 1977.
27. Marianna *Daily Times-Courier*, October 27, 1934, p. 1.

The ghoulish aftermath of the Claude Neal lynching was finally completed when Sheriff Chambliss decided to cut down Neal's body and bury it. In his official report to the governor of Florida, Chambliss stated that he "discovered" Neal's body hang-

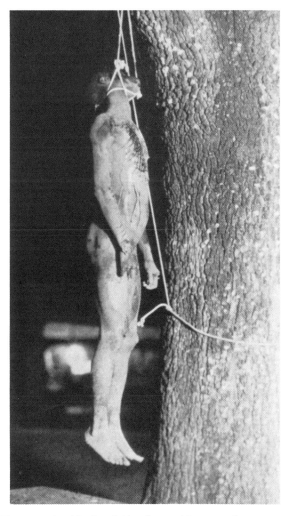

Fig. 6. Photograph of body of Claude Neal hanging from a tree near the Jackson County Courthouse, later sold as a postcard.

From NAACP, *The Lynching of Claude Neal*, courtesy of National Association for the Advancement of Colored People

ing on a tree on the courthouse grounds at 6:00 A.M. and added, "Body was cold; had been dead some time."[28]

Although the men and women who perpetrated these deeds assumed their actions would restore community order, they did so only superficially. For blacks what transpired merely confirmed their fear and mistrust of whites. Although blacks did not tell whites how they really felt about the plight of Neal at the time, they retain an oral history of the whole affair which takes exception to nearly every assumption on which the mob based its actions. They assume that Neal was trapped by circumstances. Some even conjecture that the Cannidy girl may have been "leading him on." His confession was meaningless because black prisoners could not resist pressures placed on them by white policemen. Whites saw Neal as a troublemaker and he became, therefore, a ready suspect, though no black man in Jackson County at the time was immune from these kinds of charges. And what about the rumor that a white man killed Lola Cannidy and paid Neal to change clothes with him afterwards?[29]

The lynching of Neal was just the beginning of troubles for Jackson County blacks. The tensions over the Neal incident spilled over into Saturday, October 27. Early that morning whites moved about in the business district and then headed in the direction of the courthouse square. Those who were there before 6:30 A.M. got a chance to view Neal's skinned and mutilated body. One man who saw the body confessed that he couldn't sleep for a week afterwards. But others were less agitated at the sight. Photographers were on the scene early and took hundreds of pictures of Neal's remains. They had reckoned their business investments prudently because, once the corpse was removed, disappointed late-comers were willing to pay fifty cents a photograph. These photographs were hawked in a crowd which was

28. Chambliss to Sholtz, October 31, 1934, in Lynching File, Series 278, Florida State Archives.

29. Author's interviews with several blacks in Jackson County, July 20, 1977, and with Mr. C., a black who remembers the Neal lynching, which occurred when he was a young man, and who is familiar with the stories told about it in the black community since then, December 28, 1977.

still enraged over having been left out of the spectacle when so much had been promised them; some took solace when persons in the crowd exhibited fingers and toes from Neal's body. To own them conferred genuine status. One store owner recalled the pride with which a man came into his store that morning and declared, "See what I have here." It was one of Neal's fingers.[30]

But these amenities proved insufficient for the crowd that had already become large and boisterous by 8:00 A.M. It seems likely that most of them at this stage were Jackson County riffraff and toughs from neighboring counties who had set out for Marianna just after daybreak and were now frustrated over having missed the fun. Many of them had endured also the abortive wait for Neal at the Cannidy farm, and so they felt doubly deprived. Since they had not taken part in any of the lynching rituals, their anger over Neal's supposed misdeeds was intensified. They were so vindictive toward Neal that they actually demanded that Chambliss hang the body for them one more time. Although the sheriff courageously refused all requests, the local circuit court judge, fearing that many in the crowd were armed and about to go on a rampage, prevailed upon Chambliss to allow them to view the body "in an orderly manner." The wrath of the crowd was not yet placated. The sheriff's diary entry for 9:30 A.M. was a sign of augmenting tensions: "Circuit Court adjourned on account of the mental condition of the people."

By noon there were probably more than two thousand people moving about near the courthouse; most of them would not have been there ordinarily. Many have recollections of that crowd. A man remembered that he and his brother, both young men at the time, hitchhiked seventy miles to "see something" because everyone in the whole area was talking about the lynching. He said it was easy to get a ride to Marianna that morning although more difficult to get a return ride in the evening. Still others recollect that it was not as easy to make deliveries in the business

---

30. Interview of Walter Howard with Harry Jones, June 24, 1977; Kester, "The Marianna, Florida Lynching," 4; Author's interview with Nick Pender, December 15, 1977.

section near the courthouse because groups of white people were "standing everywhere, even in the streets."[31]

Local officials blamed outsiders for the violence that followed. Mayor John Burton later declared that his community had "suffered an invasion." He informed Governor Sholtz that the responsibility lay with a "majority of not only out-of-the-city people, but from a sister state, a sister Florida county and a minority from the outlying district of our own county, with less than one per cent coming from our own city." All evidence pointed to the fact that the mayor was correct in identifying a large number of outsiders in the crowd that day.[32] The murder of the Cannidy girl and the subsequent search for and dramatic lynching of Neal had been the prime subjects of conversation throughout northwest Florida for a week, but several blacks recall wryly that there were "some familiar faces" in the crowd that tormented them during the Marianna riots of October 27.

One observer noted that feelings between blacks and whites had become more tense as the day progressed. "Slowly but steadily, almost every Negro in Marianna left the streets yesterday. Many went into hiding. Others stayed in their homes. The rest just disappeared." But not everyone was fortunate enough to hide in time. Hostility against blacks was so intense that when a white man accused a black, Bud Gammons, of starting a fight, the riot was on. According to Gammons, however, he was an innocent victim. He declared, "I was walking along the street when a white man hit me in the head. I didn't have a chance because they jumped all over me." A local newspaper described the subsequent fisticuffs, stating, "The Negro was badly beaten before being rescued by officers and taken to the sheriff's office."[33] A

31. Chambliss to Sholtz, October 31, 1934, in Lynching File, Series 278, Florida State Archives; Interview of Walter Howard with Harry Jones, June 24, 1977; Author's interview with Arthur Jensen, December 28, 1977.

32. Mayor John Burton to Governor David Sholtz, October 31, 1934, in Lynching File, Series 278, Florida State Archives; Author's interview with Doc Grant, December 29, 1977; Author's interview with several Jackson County blacks, July 20, 1977.

33. Montgomery *Advertiser*, October 28, 1934, p. 1; Tallahassee *Democrat*, October 28, 1934, p. 4; Jackson County *Floridan*, November 2, 1934, p. 8.

deputy sheriff rescued Gammons from an angry mob of about a hundred persons near the courthouse and gave him temporary asylum there in the sheriff's office. Balked in still another bid to punish blacks, the mob began to turn its frustrations on his protectors. Sheriff Chambliss appeared on the courthouse steps and vainly pleaded with the defiant group to disperse. A state supreme court justice who was visiting in Marianna may have averted a forceful entry into the courthouse and a second lynching when he also addressed the mob and insisted that Gammons' behavior, even if culpable, did not warrant summary punishment. But the angry group, two to three hundred strong, decided to make a second assault on the courthouse door. As they pummeled the door with a four-by-six-inch timber, it began to give, and law officers and other city officials trapped in the building became alarmed for their own lives. One of them retreated and locked himself in his office. Another jumped up and down to look through the transom at what the crowd was doing. He shouted at the leaders that he had a machine gun pointed directly at the door and that "if anyone broke through he was not afraid to use it on them."[34]

Between 1:30 P.M. and 4:30 P.M. that afternoon more than twenty calls were made to the governor's office by concerned persons in Marianna asking for help from the National Guard. The first call came from a besieged deputy sheriff in the courthouse who described himself as "surrounded by a mob." In the confusion of the moment constitutional formalities were set aside, and the sheriff neglected until 3:28 P.M. to make a personal call requesting the Guard as stipulated by Florida law. If the governor had waited that long to respond, it is likely that a large part of Marianna, especially its black quarters, would have been destroyed. General Collins of the Florida National Guard advised Governor Sholtz at 2:08 P.M., in response to the governor's order, that two units of militia had been assembled and that they would

34. Chambliss to Sholtz, October 31, 1934, in Lynching File, Series 278, Florida State Archives; Author's interview with Doc Grant, December 29, 1977. Grant was inside the courthouse at the time the crowd attacked it.

arrive in Marianna within three to four hours. Collins also ordered tear gas to be flown to an airport near Marianna.[35]

Even with this assurance the governor's office received one call after another from worried residents who implored immediate assistance. The local circuit judge, who called the governor from a drugstore phone booth in Marianna, was so distressed to hear from the operator that the governor's line was busy that he demanded that the operator put his call through regardless. When he was asked whether he knew whom he was attempting to interrupt, he replied that "he didn't give a damn—tell the governor's wife to get off the phone—we're having a riot out here and all hell is breaking loose." The head of the American Legion in Marianna also called Tallahassee and asked for prompt assistance. He called a second time just ten minutes later and reiterated the need for troops. A Florida state health officer residing in Marianna telephoned the governor at 2:26 P.M. to say that the situation was "bad, worse than can be imagined." The caller said he was convinced that part of the town would soon be set afire. At 2:59 P.M., Mayor Burton admonished the governor's secretary that the situation was "very serious and he needed to know when the militia was leaving." Dispatches as late as 4:25 P.M. and 4:38 P.M. reported, "Certainly need militia, are they on the way?" and "Fist fights going on spasmodically."[36]

Apparently cowed by the deputy sheriff's threat to turn a machine gun on them, the mob turned from the courthouse and discharged its fury on every black in sight. Howard Kester, who talked with eyewitnesses to the melee, wrote:

> I am reliably informed that this mob was led by a young man from Calhoun County who has money and comes from a good family. The mob apparently started from the west side of the Plaza and began driving Negroes from the streets and stores where some were engaged in buying and selling and working for white employees. An observer stated that, "the mob attacked men, women and children and that

35. Report on the Marianna riot entitled "Marianna mob," in Lynching File, Series 278, Florida State Archives.
36. Author's interview with Doc Grant, December 29, 1977; report on the Marianna riot, in Lynching File, Series 278, Florida State Archives.

several blind persons were ruthlessly beaten." Another observer said: "they [the Negroes] came from town in droves, some driving, some running, some crying, all scared to death."[37]

One black who experienced the riot simply shook his head and recalled, "It was brutal!" Another declared that it was hard for him to remember the faces of any white persons involved because he was too busy running for his life. After emptying streets and stores of blacks, the mob began to roam in the rich residential areas where black maids were employed. Altogether probably two hundred blacks suffered some form of physical punishment during the day-long riot. They were especially vulnerable because police protection collapsed everywhere. Indeed, individual policemen were themselves pursued and beaten. One of Kester's eyewitnesses declared, "The United States Army could not have stopped that crowd." City officials felt helpless because they could not locate their own policemen, and when the mayor tried to deputize special officers, he found that his offers were refused by several citizens.[38]

During the riots some individual whites courageously protected blacks, sometimes at considerable risk to themselves. Several men including a store owner and an automobile dealer calmly stepped before crowds, brandished automatic guns or rifles, and ordered the rowdies to let go of their black employees and to leave the area or be shot as trespassers. One woman who was in downtown Marianna during the riots raised such a storm when a group of marauding whites threatened her maid that the mob was scared away. Several white families in the better residential areas hid their maids; others sent cars into the Negro quarters to locate them and bring them to safety. There were also numerous helpful actions on behalf of blacks by poorer whites in the countryside. As the mob's rage disseminated into the vicinity of Marianna, one employer who owned an icehouse, three miles from the courthouse, concealed a black in a metal container that was normally used to frame three-hundred-pound blocks of ice.

37. Kester, "The Marianna, Florida Lynching," 3.
38. *Ibid.*, 5, 6.

Another white man who lived the same distance from the center of Marianna reassured the numerous blacks who lived in the fields behind him; he loaded his Winchester rifle and rocked on his front porch until calm was restored. Many blacks who were unwittingly walking toward Marianna remember whites who cautioned them that this was not a good day to go to the county seat; they would be safer at home.[39]

Economic self-interest weighed, of course, in the protection shown blacks. The man who waited with his loaded Winchester later explained, "We needed these people." One farmer who sold milk to an ice cream parlor near the courthouse saw "some white fellows reach up to get the niggers off his truck." He picked up his gun and threatened to crack their skulls. The appreciative blacks then declared, "If you work for Mr. Jensen, he will be with you" while Jensen explained later, "If you worked a nigger then you had to stand up for him." Another farmer remembered, "I was in town on that day with a truckload of peanuts when some white men came up to my truck and tried to run off the black boys who were working for me. I pulled out a .45 I had under the seat and run them off, and me and my niggers got out of town as fast as we could."[40]

Blacks who fled from Marianna sought lodging and food from relatives or friends in country areas. As one man explained, "They were running niggers out of town. Niggers couldn't be found nowhere." Many slept in the woods, the few who had guns keeping them close at hand. One black man recalls how as a boy he and his father, each with a loaded rifle, kept an all-night vigil to protect their family.[41] Blacks who lived in other towns in Jackson County responded with panic to wild reports that the mob was heading in their direction; many of them left their homes to

39. Author's interviews with Doc Grant, December 29, 1977, J. Earle Bowden, December 15, 1977, and Filmore Sims, September 27, 1977; Interview of Walter Howard with Hiram Johnson, June 13, 1977.

40. Author's interviews with Filmore Sims, September 26, 1977, and with Arthur Jensen, July 21, 1977; Interview of Walter Howard with Harry Jones, June 24, 1977.

41. Interview of Walter Howard with Harry Jones, June 24, 1977; Author's interview with Mr. C., December 28, 1977.

spend a night or two in the country. Blacks who lived as far as seventy miles away from Marianna "pulled into their houses and stayed there." One man who observed the heightened tensions between blacks and whites in distant Panama City, Florida, recalled: "Even here in Panama City niggers were afraid to come out of 'shine-town.' They were awful scared because some white folks wanted to get them awful bad. For a few days it looked bad for the niggers. There were a lot of threats to run them out of Panama City."[42]

The riots might easily have produced killings or a major conflagration had it not been for the unexpected appearance at 3:30 P.M. of a motorcade of eighty automobiles returning 350 Chicago delegates from an American Legion convention in Miami to Marianna. The legionnaires deflated the riot by staging a spectacle of their own. Their presence also deprived the rioters of anonymity, hence dominion over the city. The veterans were convoyed by eight police officers of the Florida Highway Department and three officers of the Tennessee Highway Patrol, courtesy of the governor of each state. Each driver honked his horn as he came into Marianna while each policeman pulled the siren on his motorcycle. And then in comic-opera fashion, 350 uniformed members of the American Legion stepped out of their cars in the middle of the riot; the mob became so confused it began to retreat.[43]

The first unit of the National Guard to reach Marianna was company D of the 106th Engineers from Panama City at about 4:30 P.M. They were followed by company M, 124th Infantry from Tallahassee, a total force of six officers and eighty-eight men under the command of Colonel J. P. Coombs of Apalachicola, Florida. It had required less than three hours after the request from Mayor Burton for the Guard to appear. It was fortunate that the call for troops had come on a Saturday. The National Guard cadre located their men at their normal Saturday afternoon haunts—attending ballgames, visiting local barbershops, and

---

42. Interviews of Walter Howard with Tommy Smith, July 7, 1977, and Harry Jones, June 24, 1977.
43. Montgomery *Advertiser*, October 28, 1934, p. 2.

doing house repairs. They were hastily driven to armories and issued equipment and instructions on standard riot procedures. By the time they had arrived, Colonel Coombs already had coordinated plans with local officials to suppress further mob attacks on the jail.[44]

The Guardsmen arrived by bus and were unloaded on the edge of town. The Guard's strategy was to give troublemakers a good look at troops in battle dress—helmets, rifles (1903 Springfields), pistols, packs, bayonets, and billy clubs, and so the troopers marched through town. Individual Guardsmen recall that there was still general disorder in the crowd, with small bands of men roaming the streets and looking "rough." A large crowd congregated at the edge of the courthouse square, perhaps a thousand people. Many of them taunted the soldiers with remarks such as, "Soldier boys go home!" "What business you got here?" or "We can take care of our own town."[45]

The infantry company immediately posted its men at ten- and twenty-foot intervals around the courthouse and concentrated a large number of them at the building's entrance while engineers mounted four machine guns, one at each corner of the building. Even with this display of power, some people in the crowd remained in "a rough mood." Since blacks still were being beaten up throughout Marianna, the Guard sent out patrols to assist them, usually hearing about such situations from white men who would call the courthouse. In one instance they rescued a black who was badly beaten up in the business section; one Guardsman speculates he might have been killed if the military had not intervened. That night soldiers patrolled in cars in groups of three or four, and they brought blacks into the courthouse for sanctuary. Ten to twenty blacks spent the night there. Although

44. *Report of Adjutant General of State of Florida: 1933, 1934* (Tallahassee: n.p., 1934), 20.
45. The author has spoken via telephone with five Guardsmen involved in the operation in Marianna: Jack Levins, Glenn Barrow, Hicks Jacoway, Fred Viccars, and Henry W. McMillan. He is principally indebted to the latter two troopers. McMillan was a second lieutenant at the time. He later retired from the United States Army as a general. Telephone conversation with Fred Viccars, November 15, 1977, and with Henry W. McMillan, August 6, 1977.

the weather was hot, off-duty soldiers had to sleep in a closed courthouse because they feared for the safety of blacks who were housed with them. Despite Colonel Coombs' precaution of imposing a 9:00 P.M. curfew, sporadic disorder characterized the first night including several incidents of guns firing and the stoning of houses of blacks. The next day, Sunday, October 28, incidents began to dwindle and the crowd was not as belligerent. There were fewer angry people around the courthouse and more souvenir hunters. Machine guns definitely had cooled the mob spirit, and Marianna enjoyed quiet, after eight days of turbulence. The last known act of violence associated with those days was self-inflicted. A black man who visited Marianna the day after the riots and witnessed its effects returned to Pensacola and hanged himself in the washroom of the local newspaper where he worked.[46]

The only unusual incident on Sunday was "the steady stream of visitors with cameras to the tall tree on the northeast corner of the courthouse square." The tree on which Neal's body had been displayed was the only memento of the event. Sheriff Chambliss refused that day to allow himself to be photographed and was "gruff" with newspaper correspondents.

> This whole thing has had too much notoriety already. The best thing to do is to drop the whole matter and forget it. But there's one thing you ought to know. The men who lynched that negro [Neal] ain't the men who tried to take one of my prisoners [Gammons] last night. That mob last night was led by a bunch of———rascals, and some of them were from Alabama.
>
> Now don't get me wrong. I am not saying all the leaders were from Alabama, but there were some Alabamians among the ringleaders. I like Alabama because it is a sister state. I like Alabamians too. Most of them are all right. But if any of them are figurin' on coming down here in my county and leading a mob against my jail or my deputies, they better stay up there on the other side of the state line.[47]

After these remarks the sheriff demonstrated his confidence that order had been restored. He dismissed the two National Guardsmen Colonel Coombs had assigned to protect him against

46. Author's interview with J. Earle Bowden, December 15, 1977.
47. Montgomery *Advertiser*, October 29, 1934, pp. 1, 2.

threats on his life for protecting Gammons with, "Wait at my office, boys," turned his back on reporters, glared at a photographer from a national daily, and drove off in his car.

Others were more shaken by the events and more appreciative of the stabilizing influence of the Guard. A prominent physician dispatched a letter to Governor Sholtz the day after the Guard arrived which read in part:

> Just a line to say that I have heard general expressions of appreciation from leading citizens of our county and town for the cooperation on your part in sending State militia at a time when their presence meant absolute peace and security to the citizenry of our community.
>
> I could go into detail and cite instances wherein the mob spirit had broken loose quite beyond the control of the organized authority of our city and county.
>
> It is generally stated on the streets today that had not the militia arrived yesterday afternoon that threats to burn and pillage the negro section of our town would have in all likelihood been carried out.[48]

During the early days of the next week, as the dramatic events became more remote, the major participants resumed a more normal calendar of events. Herbert Smith returned to Jackson County and the convicted bank robber and murderer Buford Mears went to prison. Neal's mother and aunt remained at Fort Barrancas near Pensacola, however, because Sheriff Chambliss feared for their safety in Jackson County.[49]

48. Dr. N. A. Baltzell to Governor David Sholtz, October 28, 1934, in Lynching File, Series 278, Florida State Archives.

49. Tallahassee *Democrat*, October 29, 1934, p. 1; Governor David Sholtz to Walter White, December 6, 1934, in Lynching File, Series 278, Florida State Archives.

Chapter 5

The Local Reaction

In view of the tumultuous events which engulfed Marianna and Jackson County on October 26 and 27, life seemingly returned to normality with astonishing rapidity. On Sunday, October 28, ministers in Jackson County reported good attendance at morning and evening services. A newsman for a Montgomery, Alabama, paper, commented the same day, "Marianna goes on her placid way apparently unaware of the drama that has attracted the attention of a nation. A waitress in a downtown cafe replied today to an inquiry as to what she thought of the excitement of the last two days, 'Well, it certainly kept us busy with so many strangers here to feed.'"[1] Howard Kester, a noted southern liberal who visited Marianna only a few days after Neal's death, observed that many citizens preferred to gloss over the violent events as if they were inevitable or even routine. He sensed that "On the whole the lynching was accepted . . . as a righteous act." Kester's views were probably partial. He was a liberal doing investigative work for the NAACP. Some church people and a number of educated citizens stated privately among themselves that they wished it hadn't happened. But as a local newspaper editor commented later, "Nobody stood up and said it should not have happened." He declared that the white people of Jackson County

1. Jackson County *Floridan*, November 2, 1934, p. 3; Montgomery *Advertiser*, October 29, 1934, p. 1.

did not condemn the outcome because "their tempers were too high; they sought vengeance for justice."[2]

Undoubtedly, Jackson County's principal officials would have preferred to see the letter of the law upheld in the Neal case. Mayor Burton did not want his city to get a reputation for lawlessness. He made a statement to a reporter from nearby Dothan, Alabama, that Marianna was "anxious to forget the occurrence and pleaded that the majority of good citizens should not suffer from the indiscretions of a few." The mayor primarily focused on Saturday's riots, which he blamed on "out-of-town agitators." He apologized for the temporary social disorder which had prevented visitors from coming to Marianna, declaring that the city had suffered an invasion:

> I am sorry to say that this [riot] caught us unprepared; we had never anticipated such an incident. I doubt there was a handful of our city people in the mob which surrounded the jail Saturday. Perhaps you won't like to hear this, but the crowd was made up mostly of Alabamians . . . a sprinkling of Georgians and people from the south end of our county. . . . I had only two policemen; to send them against that mob meant probable injuries and death for somebody; what I did was tell them to circulate among the crowd . . . and spot the leaders for later arrest, meantime holding them back as well as they could.[3]

The mayor made only a few remarks to the press about the lynching of Neal, mainly deploring the fact that Neal's body was brought to Marianna because this led to the ensuing riot. Mayor Burton also attempted to stem unfavorable publicity from national media over the Neal episode when he sent a telegram to Pathe News in New York to request that it not use numerous pictures of Jackson County taken by its cameramen. He appealed to the director of Pathe that "the outrage" had occurred "20 miles" from Marianna and did not reflect the views of the "majority of good citizens" of his city.[4]

2. Howard A. Kester, "The Marianna, Florida Lynching," 13, in Lynching File, Series 278, Florida State Archives, Tallahassee; Author's interviews with Doc Grant, June 10, 1980, and John Winslett, June 10, 1980.

3. Dothan *Eagle*, October 30, 1934, pp. 1, 2.

4. Jackson County *Floridan*, November 2, 1934, p. 1. Pathe may have destroyed the film taken of the Cannidy house and the fields and swamps nearby as well as

State's Attorney John H. Carter, a member of a prominent family in Jackson County, and a distinguished lawyer, "deplored the manner in which the Negro was punished." He wrote Governor Sholtz, "I sincerely regret that this thing has occurred in our State and especially in our county. We did our best to keep this prisoner from the mob; and the matter will be thoroughly investigated." Carter conceded, however, in an article in a local newspaper that "civil institutions must be greatly strengthened before they will supplant the lynching evil. . . . If the Scottsboro case is a living example of the law taking its course, the outlook for the suppression of the lynch law anytime soon is dismal."[5]

Sheriff Chambliss had demonstrated bravery in withholding information on Neal's whereabouts despite verbal abuse from a crowd and had taken responsible action in removing Neal from the Marianna and Chipley jails. Chambliss probably did not know that Neal was being held in the Brewton jail and this exonerated him from any complicity with the conspiracy against the victim.

Regardless of their personal sentiments, however, local officials were passive once the mob took action. In fact the law never appeared to be in serious pursuit of the mob after the initiative changed. Mayor Burton, who wished to rebuild his community's reputation, disowned responsibility by its residents. State's Attorney Carter while he "deplored the manner in which the Negro was punished" was less successful in ferreting out the perpetrators. Admittedly, his investigative tasks were not easy because as a Dothan reporter noted, "Inquiries into the lynching were likely to run into a blank wall." In reporting to Governor Sholtz, Sheriff Chambliss concluded his narrative of the lynching of Neal and the subsequent riots with the statement, "I have not been able to learn the details of the lynching, and so do not know whether he [Neal] was killed in Alabama or Florida. I am making further in-

---

that taken in Marianna. Sherman Grinberg Studios in New York currently owns most Pathe film from the 1930s, but it does not retain any material on the Neal lynching.

5. John H. Carter to Governor David Sholtz, October 27, 1934, in Official Correspondence of Governor David Sholtz, Florida State Archives.

vestigations along this line and will advise you of results." Subsequent investigation apparently proved unrewarding because no new evidence came to the governor's desk. The county coroner displayed similar inertia. As of October 28, he had not called an inquest into Neal's death, and he reportedly stated that "he did not know whether he would." The coroner's report is missing from the Jackson County courthouse. If written, it undoubtedly was destroyed.[6]

What explained this ineffectual prosecution of the mob which killed Neal? The critical factor was that while many people in Jackson County would have preferred a jury trial for Neal, they were not sufficiently militant to initiate action against the lynchers. The effective will to prosecute a lynch mob or those in seeming conspiracy with them, the leaders of the vigil at the Cannidy farm, all highly visible, was not present. One man close to the scene declared that if people had taken time to think probably 90 percent of local citizens would have condemned what happened. But under the circumstances of anger and swift execution of reprisals, even ministers, churches, and newspapers remained officially silent.[7] Local blacks meanwhile were terrified and anxious to remain on good terms with all whites. Many of them were probably happy just to be alive.

Jackson County officials were probably concerned lest their investigations would result in confrontations which would simply lead to more social unrest. Even after the situation had calmed and the National Guard was withdrawn, they were still apprehensive that new outbreaks of violence might occur. Mayor Burton was fearful that troubles might return the next Saturday night and Sheriff Chambliss took special precautions to swear in a number of extra deputies. There were also unconfirmed rumors that the FERA Purification League would demonstrate against

6. Dothan *Eagle*, October 30, 1934, pp. 1, 5; Sheriff W. Flake Chambliss to Governor David Sholtz, October 31, 1934, in Lynching File, Series 278, Florida State Archives; Tallahassee *Democrat*, October 28, 1934, p. 4; Author's interview with Mr. A., December 15, 1977.
7. Author's interviews with Doc Grant and John Winslett, both June 10, 1980.

blacks who were on the relief rolls, to purge the lists for white applicants. As late as November 17, 1934, nearly a month after the killing of Lola Cannidy, Sheriff Chambliss advised Governor Sholtz it would still be unwise for Neal's aunt and mother to return to Marianna from Pensacola.[8]

Newspapers within seventy-five miles of Marianna supported their neighbors with positive editorial opinion on the lynching despite blistering criticism from the "outside press." The only extant editorial in Marianna's papers is in the *Daily Times-Courier* of November 8, 1934. It quotes approvingly another editorial in the Panama City *Pilot* and concludes with its own comment:

> Why plead clemency for a diabolical criminal and fiend, who confessed to his crime and at the same time gave the world a clear conception his victim had neither a chance to call for help nor a weapon of defense. Here is just cause why a community was stirred and maddened with grim determination to avenge the insult to womanhood. This was the real reason why hundreds of men left their work and joined in the hunt, with only one object in view—to hunt the criminal, find him if it consumed all of a year, and mete unmerciful torture to him, as he did to a young girl. . . .
>
> The above editorial appeared in the Panama City *Pilot*. The editor is Mrs. Sadie West, and she went to Panama City some years ago from a state far above the Mason and Dixon Line. The sentiment expressed in her editorial is exactly the same as would be of many of those north of us who would not criticize us . . . if they were to live here themselves. In fact, we seriously doubt the sincerity of some of the editors in their scathing condemnation of the good people of Jackson county. We can not stretch our imagination to think that any good American citizen anywhere, of any color or creed, could be other than enraged to the extreme if the unspeakable crime was committed upon the fair womanhood of their community. . . . When we read some of their "masterpieces" on the subject we are constrained to say, in the words of our Saviour, "Forgive them Father, they know not what they do."[9]

The Panama City *Pilot*'s most enthusiastic support came in an

---

8. Minutes of the City Council, Marianna, Florida, October 29, 1934, p. 1; Tallahassee *Democrat*, November 3, 1934, p. 1; Chambliss to Sholtz, November 17, 1934, in Lynching File, Series 278, Florida State Archives.

9. Marianna *Daily Times-Courier*, November 8, 1934, p. 2.

editorial published the night Neal was lynched. The editor declared that act was "Avenging an Insult": "What America needs today is men who are willing to defend virtue and womanhood, not only against the brute Negro, but the social temptations of today that are placed around our girls." The nearby DeFuniak Springs *Herald* responded similarly on November 1, 1934, declaring that lynching was merely the conventional punishment for the rape of a white woman by a black man.[10]

Editorials from newspapers outside northwest Florida were uniformly critical of recent events there. This response appeared in most papers either on Saturday, October 27, or Sunday, October 28, because of the advance notice on the lynching released by AP on October 26. The Tampa *Tribune*, on October 28, blamed lax laws and faulty enforcement. The editor of the Richmond *Times-Dispatch* feared that the Neal affair might signal a return to the barbarities against blacks practiced earlier in the South:

> The barbarous affair which occurred Friday night in Florida is a blot on Southern civilization which cannot be erased. We Southerners pride ourselves on our manners and mores, and yet we permit such incredible exhibitions of sadistic frenzy to occur in our midst. . . .
>
> Apparently the South is lapsing into the interracial barbarities of several decades ago.

The Birmingham, Alabama, *News-Age-Herald* also spoke for the urban South when its editor wrote, "Any lynching is hideous; but this one was peculiarly hideous."[11]

Editorials in major American newspapers heaped criticism on the state of Florida and its inhabitants as much as the lynch mob. On October 29, a Washington *Post* lead editorial censured state government in Florida for its ineffectual response to mob rule. Another lead editorial on the lynching in the Baltimore *Sun* titled "Ha, Ha!" took satisfaction from the fact that the perversities of the Florida crowd at the Cannidy farm had backfired and deprived them of their gratifications. An editorial writer in the Boston

10. Panama City *Pilot*, October 25, 1934, p. 2; DeFuniak Springs *Herald*, November 1, 1934, p. 2.

11. Tampa *Tribune*, October 28, 1934, p. 4; Richmond *Times-Dispatch*, October 28, 1934, p. 2; Birmingham *News-Age-Herald*, October 28, 1934, p. 4.

Herald suggested sardonically that Florida might now exploit lynchings as a new tourist resource.[12]

Florida's governor, David Sholtz, became a special target for editorial criticism when the state took no action against the lynchers despite Sholtz's disclosure that "some of the ringleaders of the mob are supposed to be known." The Richmond *Times-Dispatch* wrote an accusatory editorial on November 5, 1934, entitled, "Going After Mobsters."

> It was assumed, especially after the wave of indignation that swept the country that in Alabama or Florida, or both, a Grand Jury would inquire into the savage lynching of a Negro on Florida soil more than a week ago. . . .
> The point is: If the Governor or others in authority know who these ringleaders are, why don't they act to jail the suspects?[13]

Pressures on Sholtz had come even before Neal's execution when it seemed there was still time to save his life. Will W. Alexander, the executive director of the Commission on Interracial Cooperation had wired Sholtz at 2:54 P.M. on October 26, about eight hours before Neal died. He informed Sholtz where and when the lynching would occur and "urgently requested him to take all possible steps to avert the threatened crime."[14] At 5:46 P.M., Mrs. William P. Cornell, the Florida state chairman of the Association of Southern Women to Prevent Lynching, dispatched a telegram to Sholtz reading, COLD BLOODED PROSPECTIVE LYNCHING OF NEGRO . . . TONIGHT TOO HORRIBLE TO CONTEMPLATE. She implored the governor to call out troops in keeping with his previous promise to her to have the National Guard ready for deterrent action against lynchers on two-hour notice.[15] If this policy

12. Washington *Post*, October 29, 1934, p. 6; Baltimore *Evening Sun*, October 27, 1934, p. 6; Boston *Herald*, October 29, 1934, p. 10.

13. Richmond *Times-Dispatch*, November 5, 1934, p. 6.

14. W. W. Alexander to Governor David Sholtz, October 26, 1934, in Lynching File, Series 278, Florida State Archives.

15. Mrs. W. P. Cornell to Governor David Sholtz, October 26, 1934, in Lynching File, Series 278, Florida State Archives. Mrs. Cornell had previously acknowledged Governor Sholtz's "promise" to prevent lynching in Florida by calling out the National Guard within two hours of notification. See Jeannie D. M. Cornell to the Honorable David Sholtz, January 31, 1934, in Florida Files, Association of Southern Women to Prevent Lynching Papers, Trevor-Arnett Library, Atlanta University, Atlanta, Georgia.

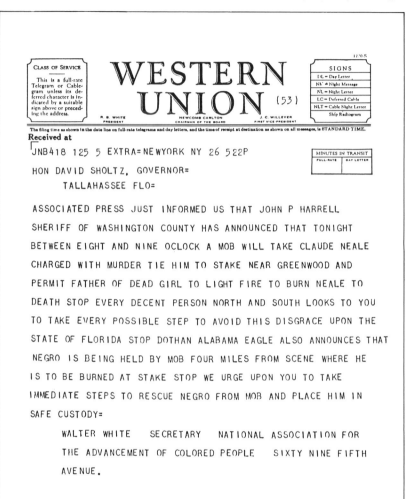

Fig. 7. Walter White's telegram to Governor David Sholtz urging that Neal's lynching be prevented.

Courtesy of Florida State Archives, Tallahassee, Lynching File, Series 278

had been implemented, there would have been time to save Neal. Walter White, secretary of the NAACP, had sent a similar telegram to Sholtz only minutes earlier (see Fig. 7).[16]

After the lynching more than one hundred telegrams and letters arrived at the governor's office, mostly from persons who condemned Sholtz for permitting the lynching or who called upon him to prosecute its perpetrators. Most complainants represented small organizations such as ministerial alliances, church leagues, young people's groups, and individual YWCAs. But the Christian Council of Churches and left-wing pressure groups such as the Scottsboro Defense Fund, the New York International Labor Defense, and the Philadelphia District of the Young Communist League also contacted Sholtz. Vito Marcantonio, the liberal congressman from New York's twentieth congressional district, wired Sholtz on October 27 to "hold you responsible for your deliberate failure to maintain law and order." One of the most interesting denunciatory telegrams came from a writers' organization. It was signed by such distinguished figures as Stephen V. Benet, Van Wyck Brooks, Erskine Caldwell, Theodore Dreiser, E. Franklin Frazier, Louis M. Hacker, James Weldon Johnson, Freda Kirchway, Joseph Wood Krutch, Sinclair Lewis, Lewis Mumford, George Jean Nathan, Robert Nathan, Upton Sinclair, and Carl Van Doren.[17]

Governor Sholtz also received numerous letters from individuals who read accounts of the incident in newspapers using the AP national wire, including the New York *Times* on its front page of October 28, 1934.[18] A few of these letters congratulated the gov-

16. Walter White to Governor David Sholtz, October 26, 1934, in Lynching File, Series 278, Florida State Archives.

17. Samuel McCrea Calvert to Governor David Sholtz, October 30, 1934, Vito Marcantonio to Governor David Sholtz, October 27, 1934, and W. E. Woodard (Chairman, Writer's League), and Secretary Suzanne LaFollette to Governor David Sholtz, October 28, 1934, all in Lynching File, Series 278, Florida State Archives.

18. Some of the newspapers which ran descriptions of the mob's plans were the Atlanta *Constitution*, Birmingham *News*, Boston *Herald*, Cincinnati *Enquirer*, Kansas City *Star*, Louisville *Courier-Journal*, Milwaukee *Sentinel*, Peoria *Journal*, Richmond *Times-Dispatch*, and at least seven other papers, which demonstrated that, as the NAACP later claimed, "All of America Knew of Lynching in Advance." See National Association for the Advancement of Colored People,

Fig. 8. Collage of newspaper headlines later put together by NAACP dramatizing advance notice of Neal's fate.

From NAACP, *The Lynching of Claude Neal,* courtesy of National Association for the Advancement of Colored People

ernor for protecting the country's morals, one noting that America would be safeguarded only "as long as we kept the Negroes and the Romanists under control."[19] Another supporter, a Florida woman, sent Sholtz a copy of a letter she had forwarded to Mrs. Cornell, chairman of the Florida chapter of the ASWPL:

> In this morning's paper I read of your sending a telegram to call out the troops in defense of Neal, the negro brute that assaulted and mutilated the body of a white girl. How could you a white woman ask such a request? Suppose it was a female of your family met with such a fate, would you wait for troops? Oh, no, you would cry out for vengeance. I pray the Southern men will always stand shoulder to shoulder for White Supremacy, and clear the earth of such reptiles as Neal and his kind, by rope, fire or anything at hand. You let the negroes think that they are somebody, and you will have a job on your hands hard to get rid of. I cannot comprehend a Southern woman (if you are one) coming out in defense of a low down nigger. Wake up. . . . Stand firmly for White Supremacy, right or wrong, White Supremacy. I wish I was eloquent enough to express myself more forcibly.[20]

The majority of letter writers, however, disapproved of the incident and of the ineffective preventive steps taken by civil authorities. One man acknowledged that he had removed himself from Florida immediately after the Neal incident and had "returned to New York and civilization." He hoped that the lynching would contribute to a slump in Florida's tourist season. A woman admonished that her family would not be coming this year on this account.[21] Many letters from whites from all parts of the country expressed outrage. A New Yorker wrote:

> I am a white man, a manager of a book shop in New York City—but damned if I don't feel ashamed of belonging to the same race as the sadistic savages who are holding the negro, Claude Neal . . . and have announced his promised torture and burning alive. . . .

The Lynching of Claude Neal (New York: n.p., 1934), 3, in Lynching File, Series 278, Florida State Archives. See also Fig. 8.

19. H. H. Warner to Governor David Sholtz, October 27, 1934, in Lynching File, Series 278, Florida State Archives.

20. E. J. Humphries to Governor David Sholtz, October 27, 1934, in Lynching File, Series 278, Florida State Archives.

21. Tom Rempests to Governor David Sholtz, December 5, 1934, and Mrs. George Trenholen to Governor David Sholtz, December 4, 1934, both in Lynching File, Series 278, Florida State Archives.

THE MOB GIVES ADVANCE NOTICE TO THE LAW   —*By Jerry Doyle.*

Fig. 9. Cartoon by Jerry Doyle published two days after the lynching.
From Philadelphia *Record*, October 29, 1934, courtesy of Free Public Library, Philadelphia

If you permit those pitiable sadists to have their type of "fun" at the expense of this Negro who is accused of killing one of your so precious white girls, I rank you among that rotten scum. If you have average human feelings, I urge you to intervene at once.[22]

After the lynching occurred, the Florida governor received more irate letters such as one from a man in Plainwell, Michigan:

What are a murderer's last thoughts before he goes to sleep at night. . . . Does a Southern "gentleman" at last become so accustomed to

22. Unsigned letter to Governor David Sholtz, November 11, 1934, in Lynching File, Series 278, Florida State Archives.

brutality that he is immune to any humanitarian feelings? Of course, I realize that to you a "nigger" is probably less deserving of pity than a dog but could any decent man stand by and see a dog mutilated, burned, shot, kicked and hanged without making any attempt to save its life?

My father fought during the Civil War for the freedom of the Negro. He and his cause have quite evidently failed and his son's only means of protest is this weak letter which will probably go unread.[23]

Blacks expressed a variety of opinions, some imploring the governor to assure effective prosecution of the culprits, others expressing disillusionment with American justice, and still others threatening retaliation. A group of ministers of the African Methodist Episcopal church near Hastings, Florida, appealed to the governor's and the state's sense of pride to bring the lynchers to justice in order to "erase this black mark which the people of Florida have unjustly been given by those who have no love for their state, no respect for law and order and no concern for the sensibilities of their fellowmen." One group, which represented itself as the Negro Welfare League WXYZ writing from Savannah, Georgia, warned Sholtz that unless those guilty of the crimes against Neal were found, "we will poison river branches and wells and burn enough property and kill enough to pay for Neal's death." The writer asked, "Since white men have no respect for the law why should we?" He vowed, "If you failed to get the guilty ones we will get them by some means."[24]

The theme of disillusionment with whites was stated with poignancy in a letter from a black man in West Palm Beach, Florida:

I feel quite sure that after you shall have read my letter through, you will pardon my interruption of your valuable time. I shall attempt to make this as direct as possible.

As you recall the awful lynching of the twenty-one year old Negro near Marianna, Fla., it seems hardly necessary for me to go into detail regarding this affair. The lynching of that Negro in the manner in

23. Harry Preller to Governor David Sholtz, October 27, 1934, in Lynching File, Series 278, Florida State Archives. Governor Sholtz did reply to the letter.

24. Leonard F. Morse (for the Ministerial Alliance) to Governor David Sholtz, October 29, 1934, and Negro Welfare League to Governor David Sholtz, November 14, 1934, both in Lynching File, Series 278, Florida State Archives.

which the act was committed did something to me that I had hoped would never happen. I presume by now that you have already guessed that I am a Negro, and I must say I am proud of it. I am more than that; I am southern born—born and reared in Georgia, the State of which I am still proud even though she has been ridiculed, to the people of America.

I was reared by a true, constant and devout Christian mother, who taught me to love and respect the white race. All my life I have had beautiful dreams of a white's man character; of his standard of right and justice; of his desire to be fair and just by all mankind regardless of color or creed. THESE ARE THE BEAUTIFUL THINGS MY BLACK MOTHER TAUGHT ME. But today I have been sadly disillusioned. . . .

You will recall, Honorable Sir, that we were brought here in 1620 without any choice on our part to serve you. This we have done without complaint for 314 years. We find today, that after having served and honored you through all these trying years, we are being supplanted by every other race on earth. We have fought for you, we have died for you and have never yet tried to overthrow the government, and yet we are being treated worse than any people. . . . We are asking for protection, the same protection that you would give anyone else, not murder us because our skin is black; for murder it is in the sight of God. Let us be tried and if we are found guilty, punish us to the "Nth" degree, the same as you would anyone else.

Honorable Sir, restore my faith in the white man of America and let me feel that the flag that my two brothers defended protects me as much as it does anyone. I had a classmate who was shot from the flag pole raising "Ol' Glory." Let me feel that he did not die in vain.

Very respectfully,
M. B. Collie [25]

Governor David Sholtz (1891–1952), a colorful, cheerful, cigar-smoking politician, was well suited to the needs of Floridians during the early years of the Depression.[26] He identified closely with Franklin Roosevelt and the New Deal and prided himself on

25. M. B. Collie to Governor David Sholtz, November 12, 1934, in Lynching File, Series 278, Florida State Archives. Another letter by a black which cites the injustice of blacks shedding their blood for whites in World War I but then being denied "decent protection of the law" is unsigned letter (Cincinnati) to Governor David Sholtz, November 12, 1934, in Lynching File, Series 278, Florida State Archives.

26. For interpretations of Sholtz, see Merlin G. Cox, "David Sholtz: New Deal Governor of Florida," *Florida Historical Quarterly*, XLIII (1964), 142–52. The official papers of Governor Sholtz are located at the Florida State Archives, Tallahassee, Florida.

the amount of federal relief allocations Florida received from 1932 through 1936 while he was governor. Sholtz was a rhetorical rather than practical liberal. He spent federal monies but regarded the balanced state budget as his most salutary achievement. Actually federal monies were a source of ruin for his administration, which suffered from political favoritism and corruption because Sholtz, a genial man, could not manage his own political supporters.

His attitude on questions of minority rights is difficult to establish, but his background as the son of Jewish immigrants who lived in New York would suggest positive action, and his pledge to Florida leaders of the ASWPL to send the National Guard within two hours of notification to the site of a prospective lynching promised as much. Sholtz first received news of the mob's intent to take Neal's life at 6:30 P.M. after a phone call from his secretary reached him in Arcadia, Florida, where the governor had stopped for the night en route from Miami to Tallahassee. He immediately phoned Sheriff Chambliss, who gave the governor "every assurance that he could cope with the situation and did not require outside assistance." Technically, under Florida law, a sheriff had to request the National Guard before soldiers could be dispatched, and so the case was closed. But once he heard Neal had been killed by the mob, Sholtz found it necessary to establish other reasons for not summoning troops. He explained, "There was nothing that could have been done to prevent the lynching of the Negro after it was called to my attention. It was not a case of calling out the militia to protect the jail or a prisoner in custody of an officer. The Negro was held in the hands of a mob out in the woods where he was killed. Under existing circumstances it would have been futile to have called out the militia."[27]

Sholtz perceived that the cruel murder of Neal had touched off a national furor and that public opinion would not be placated by clichés about the governor's inability to act without the sheriff's assent. Sholtz, of course, might have declared martial law and

27. Tallahassee *Democrat*, October 28, 1934, p. 1.

sent the troops regardless of the sheriff. Perhaps as a consequence of the bombardment of letters and telegrams reaching his desk, Sholtz soon issued another statement. Its wording is interesting because Sholtz further absolved himself for his inactivity by gratuitously declaring that Neal was guilty. He asserted:

> This lynching was not only deplorable but absolutely unnecessary in this state under the present administration, where crimes of this character are so speedily and summarily dealt with. As an example, the negro, Doc Williams, who committed a similar crime on August 24th last was arrested on September 5th, convicted on September 22nd, the death warrant signed by the Governor on October 2nd and he was executed on October 8th. Thus in a perfectly orderly and legal manner and with credit to the State this man paid the penalty of his crime, in thirty-three days after he was apprehended and only forty-five days after the crime was committed. There is absolutely no excuse for mob law in a State which deals so promptly with criminals of this character.[28]

Governor Sholtz also announced that he had asked State's Attorney Carter for a "thorough and searching investigation into this matter" and Sheriff Chambliss for a "complete report."[29] He said that his actions would be contingent on the substance of those reports and "further independent investigation which had been ordered." He also requested that both the state's attorney and the sheriff appear before him personally on October 30.

At that conference Sholtz said to Chambliss, "What disturbs me is reports that notice of its intentions were given by the mob when it took the Negro from the Alabama jail." When the governor asked Chambliss what he did to rescue Neal, the sheriff replied, "We tried to surround Jackson County with deputies but we never did see the mob." Later the governor told the sheriff, who had submitted a lengthy chronology of the Neal lynching, "It looked from first reports that you had not exerted every effort to protect the prisoner, but I am convinced from your reports that you did all you possibly could."

28. For the formal statement by Governor Sholtz on Neal lynching, see Sholtz Correspondence, October 27, 1934, in Florida State Archives.
29. Tallahassee *Democrat*, November 1, 1934, p. 1.

Turning to State's Attorney Carter, Governor Sholtz declared: "We don't condone lynching in Florida. I want you and the Grand Jury to make a vigorous and thorough effort to run down the ringleaders of this mob and prosecute them. It has been reported to me that some of the ringleaders are supposed to be known."[30]

While awaiting the results of the grand jury probe, Sholtz took steps to repair his position with critics who felt more effective initiative on his part could have averted the incident. On November 1, 1934, he restated his position on why troops were not called out to protect Neal: civil authorities in Jackson County did not ask for the troops. Besides, to have sent them would have been futile. He elaborated the reasoning behind the latter contention:

> The Colonel in charge of the troops that were sent to Marianna Saturday made an investigation and yesterday gave his report to the Governor to the effect that calling the militia the preceding night would have been futile, as the Negro was held by the mob in the woods, presumably right at the State line where they could have jumped back across into Alabama at the approach of the troops, if the troops had been able to locate them. Or else they would have immediately killed the Negro upon the approach of troops, if indeed he had not already been killed by the mob. Sending troops to Marianna on Friday night would have been like the ill-fated Pershing expedition into Mexico after Villa.[31]

The governor's analysis may be questioned. If Neal were held near the Alabama line, then the problem of locating him would have been substantially reduced. It seems doubtful that members of the mob would have taken him back into Alabama because they had made elaborate promises to deliver him to the Cannidys. And the assertion that the mob would have killed Neal if they knew troops were on the way was conjectural. His fate in the hands of the mob was hardly a better one.

On November 10, State's Attorney Carter sent Sholtz a copy of the Jackson County grand jury's findings on Neal's death. Part of that statement declared:

30. *Ibid.*, 8.
31. Governor David Sholtz to Mrs. Walter S. Jones, November 1, 1934, in Lynching File, Series 278, Florida State Archives.

> We have not been able to get much direct or positive evidence with reference to this matter; practically all of our evidence and information being in the nature of hearsay and rumors. However, we find that Miss Cannidy was brutally raped and murdered in this county on the 18th day of October, 1934, by Claud [sic] Neal, a negro and that Claud [sic] Neal came to his death in this county on the 26th day of October, 1934, at the hands of a small group of persons unknown to us; after being forcibly removed from the jail at Brewton, Alabama, about 175 miles from here, by persons unknown to us.
>
> We find that the Sheriff of our county did everything within his power under the circumstances to protect his prisoner, and we commend him for his action in performing his duty.
>
> We do not think anything can be accomplished by remaining in session longer at this time, but we are ready and willing to continue our investigation of this matter at any time additional evidence of a convincing and substantial nature can be presented to us.
>
> In view of the situation, we ask that we now be dismissed, subject to being recalled for further action.[32]

It was ironic that the grand jury's probe which was unable to obtain "much direct or positive evidence" in so public a matter as Neal's death was able to state categorically that Miss Cannidy, who met her horrible death alone, was the victim of Neal's outrages. By its inclusion of a statement of Neal's guilt in what was an inquiry designed to establish the causes of his death, the jury had performed a tour de force. In effect, it not only exonerated Neal's lynchers but provided a justification for their deeds. It seems likely that evidence against the lynchers was fragmentary. Whether the prosecuting officer, Carter, obtained information for the jury is unknown also. It is doubtful if the investigation was ever intended to be more than perfunctory. Since the state's attorney promised Sholtz, in a covering letter, that he would recall the grand jury if he obtained additional evidence, and since that body was not reconvened, one must assume that Carter failed to turn up additional information of significance.

Although letters and telegrams pressuring Sholtz to pursue a vigorous inquiry into the incident had slackened by November

32. John H. Carter to David Sholtz, November 10, 1934, in Lynching File, Series 278, Florida State Archives.

12, when he received Carter's report, Walter White, secretary of the NAACP, was still peppering him with calls for more effective action. Sholtz had replied to White's telegram with a letter dated October 27, restating his regrets over the lynching and his inability to save Neal.[33] On October 30, White had replied, chiding Sholtz for not hearing about Neal's plight until 6:30 P.M. when White himself knew in New York at 3:00 P.M. White persisted, arguing that even if Sholtz did not learn what was going on until 6:30 P.M. he still had more than three hours to move troops to defend Neal.[34]

On November 22, White sent Sholtz a copy of the investigation of the Neal lynching by Howard Kester. Kester's leads on persons supposedly responsible for the lynching were passed on to State's Attorney Carter in Marianna. The latter replied, "From what information I have been able to gather concerning the lynching of Claud [*sic*] Neal, I find this report to be grossly inaccurate, extremely exaggerated and founded mainly upon false rumors floating about the county." The attorney's use of terms like "grossly inaccurate" and "extremely exaggerated" imply norms and data which were not in the governor's hands, but Sholtz did not pursue the subjects with him further. Carter took particular exception to Kester's opinion that Neal and Lola Cannidy had been sexually intimate ("That portion of Kester's report alleging an immoral relationship . . . I brand as a lie of the whole cloth"). On November 24, White wrote once more to Governor Sholtz. Since Sholtz had repeatedly declared his opposition to mob actions against persons, White asked him to sign a petition with other governors, mayors, churchmen, and business leaders to support an antilynching bill to be presented in Congress in the early part of 1935. When Sholtz did not comply, he wired the governor on December 21, nearly a month after a text of the bill had been forwarded, and asked Sholtz to authorize his signature in support

33. Governor David Sholtz to Walter White, October 27, 1934, in Lynching File, Series 278, Florida State Archives.
34. Walter White to Governor David Sholtz, October 30, 1934, in Lynching File, Series 278, Florida State Archives.

by December 26. White received merely a noncommittal reply
from Sholtz's secretary.[35]

If Marianna newspapers are indicative, Jackson County by mid-
November had returned to normal. On November 16, the lynching was chiefly remembered by a headline, "Lynching of Negro
Brings News of Brother Missing More Than Generation." Sheriff
Chambliss' brother had reestablished contact with him as a result of reading about the mob action in Jackson County in a Cali-
fornia newspaper. A writer for the local paper declared in the
same issue, "Excitement of Jackson County's recent lynching has
died down and the smoke of inter-racial tension has to a great
extent cleared away."[36]

35. John H. Carter to Governor David Sholtz, November 10, 1934, Walter
White to Governor David Sholtz, November 24, 1934, and J. P. Newell to Walter
White, December 21, 1934, all in Lynching File, Series 278, Florida State Archives.
36. Jackson County *Floridan*, November 16, 1934, pp. 1, 7.

Chapter 6

The National Conscience

Mr. President, our organization is appealing to you and your New Deal to give or say a word in behalf of the eighteen or more millions of Negroes in this United States. . . . Mr. President, if there's anything that you can do without hurting your influence with the dominant race, it would certainly be a God-send to the Negroes equal to that of the late honorable President Abraham Lincoln.

Alton Wright, Superintendent of Colored Rescue Mission, New York, to President Roosevelt, on October 25, 1934, two days before Claude Neal was lynched.

The lynchers who seized Neal and returned him to Florida across the Alabama state boundary never gave a second thought to possible federal prosecution. And newspapers in Jackson County at the time made no mention of reprisals by federal law enforcement agencies. Indeed, through federal relief and crop programs, twentieth-century Jackson countians were probably becoming aware of the impact of the national government on their daily lives for the first time.

There had been no mention in either of the local newspapers of the proposed federal antilynching legislation in the early months of 1934. The Wagner-Costigan Bill of 1934 (S. 1978) sought to intimidate mobs from lynchings by imposing stiff penalties. It defined a mob "as a group of three or more persons, lacking a legal basis who set about to harm another or deprive him of life."[1] The bill was to come into effect "in the event the state or governmental subdivision should fail to protect its citizens." It provided a fine of up to five thousand dollars and a maximum jail sentence of five years or both for a state or local official who "failed to protect his citizens or to arrest or prosecute violators of the law." Other major provisions extended jurisdiction to federal district courts to enter a suspected lynching case if county or state courts

1. *Congressional Record*, 73rd Cong., 2nd Sess., 1820–21.

115

failed to initiate action after thirty days and imposed a fine of ten thousand dollars on the county in which the lynching occurred.

The NAACP became the chief pressure group in support of the bill, which probably obtained majority backing in Congress.[2] The NAACP had decided to resume leadership in what had been one of its major causes in the 1920s for several reasons. Lynchings, the most violent and flagrant affront to the black man's equality in America, were on the increase after 1933, and the NAACP could ill afford to allow radical groups to preempt its leadership.[3] Besides, Walter White, successor of James Weldon Johnson as executive secretary of the NAACP, felt that his organization would benefit from support of the president and Mrs. Roosevelt.[4] Light-skinned, a polished conversationalist, writer, and socializer, White relished working for the social amelioration of blacks in causes which enlisted the brightest and the best of both races. In addition, there were deep personal reasons for White's espousal of the antilynching cause. A conversation with White sooner or later turned to lynching, as Eleanor Roosevelt once noted in a letter to presidential aide Steve Early.[5]

In addition to the organizational strength of NAACP and the able leadership of Senators Wagner and Costigan, the president's support helped chances for passage of the antilynching bill. Roosevelt had offered explicit backing in his annual message to Congress on January 3, 1934, when he declared: "Crimes of organized banditry, cold blooded shooting, lynching and kidnapping have threatened our security. These violations of ethics and these violations of law call on the strong arm of the government for their immediate suppression; they call also on the country for an

2. Walter White to Marvin H. McIntyre, April 14, 1934, in Presidential Papers, Official File 93-A, Franklin D. Roosevelt Library, Hyde Park, New York.

3. Walter White to Franklin D. Roosevelt (telegram), December 30, 1933, in Presidential Papers, Official File 93-A, Roosevelt Library. White wrote: "The wave of mob murders during 1933 requires drastic remedy. Many Americans feel Congress should pass Anti-lynching Bill."

4. See White's résumé of meeting with Roosevelts in his letter to the president, May 11, 1934, in Presidential Papers, Official File 93-A, Roosevelt Library.

5. Eleanor Roosevelt to Steve Early, August 8, 1935, in Eleanor Roosevelt Papers, Series 100, 1411, Franklin D. Roosevelt Library, Hyde Park, New York.

aroused public opinion."[6] President Roosevelt also welcomed Walter White for an interview at the White House. White used the occasion to point out that an antilynching bill would not only help Negroes but the image of the entire country as a statement of human rights against the Nazi and Fascist movements. According to White's recollections, the president "expressed keen interest in and knowledge of the facts regarding lynching and reiterated his abhorrence of the evil."[7] At the close of the interview, Roosevelt promised White that he would consult with Senators Costigan and Wagner and "would urge upon the leaders of Congress that the Bill be brought up and voted upon before Congress adjourns." FDR fulfilled all his promises to White though the bill never came to a vote.[8] The president thereupon, however, wrote a consoling note to White asking him to persevere: "No one can glance even casually at the progress which Negroes have achieved in the past sixty years, particularly in the last fifteen years since the end of World War I without finding hope and inspiration for the future."[9] The Claude Neal lynching, coming just after the failure of a hopeful campaign for antilynching legislation and just before the advent of a new congressional session in January, 1935, rekindled aspirations for another legislative effort. White sensed the Neal episode might become the Dreyfus case of the antilynching movement. It provided him with a national sounding board.[10] Major newspapers and several radio stations had described its events on October 27 or 28, and some, including the New York *Times*, devoted front-page coverage. Editorials con-

6. New York *Times*, January 4, 1934, p. 2.

7. Walter White to Judge Irving Lehman, May 9, 1934, in National Association for the Advancement of Colored People (NAACP) Papers, I, C-154, Manuscript Division, Library of Congress; Walter White to President Franklin D. Roosevelt, May 11, 1934, in Presidential Papers, Official File 93-A, Roosevelt Library.

8. Louis Howe with FDR's authorization informed Oscar de Priest, black congressman from Illinois, that the president encouraged a vote on Wagner-Costigan before adjournment. See Louis Howe to Oscar de Priest, June 15, 1934, in Presidential Papers, Official File 93-A, Roosevelt Library.

9. Franklin D. Roosevelt to Walter White, June 22, 1934, in Presidential Papers, President's Public File 1336, Roosevelt Library.

10. Walter White to Honorable Isabelle Greenway, January 25, 1936, in NAACP Papers, I, C-251.

demning Neal's fate appeared in numerous papers, one from the Richmond *Times-Dispatch* speculating that the Neal lynching "served greatly to increase the chances for anti-lynch legislation."[11]

White was heartened by the response of the media for, as his correspondence showed, the Neal lynching had affected him deeply. He once called it "one of the most bestial crimes ever committed by a mob" and another time "perhaps the most gruesome of all lynchings." In another letter he wrote, "Nothing has ever sickened me like the Marianna lynching and everytime I hear or read it, it makes me just as ill as the first time."[12] To Mrs. Roosevelt he confided, "I have been sick at heart ever since the revelation of what actually occurred [in Greenwood]."[13]

White moved quickly to mobilize public opinion to exert public pressures on the Justice Department, the president, and the Congress. Simultaneously, he applied pressures on them himself. Immediately after White learned that Neal had been murdered, he telegrammed information to wire services, leading radio commentators, the editors of New York newspapers, the seventy NAACP branches, and the New York correspondent of the London *Herald*.[14] On that same day he wired President Roosevelt asking him "to put the Costigan-Wagner Bill in his 'Must Program' for the next session."[15] He also contacted Attorney General

11. New York *Times*, October 28, 1934, p. 1. A very complete record of newspaper editorials on the Neal incident may be found in Lynching Records, Boxes 29 and 30, Tuskegee Institute Archives, Tuskegee, Alabama. *Scholastic*, the national high school weekly, also described some details of the lynching and appealed to the astonishment of its youthful audience with the comment, "It happened not in the heart of primitive Africa, but . . . in the civilized United States." *Scholastic Magazine*, XXV (November 17, 1934), 21.
12. Walter White to William Rosenwald, November 16, 1934, in NAACP Papers, I, C-78; Walter White to T. M. Durlach, November 23, 1934, in NAACP Papers, I, C-207; Walter White to Carl Van Vechten, December 14, 1934, in NAACP Papers, I, C-154.
13. Walter White to Eleanor Roosevelt, November 27, 1934, in Eleanor Roosevelt Papers, Series 100, 1325, Roosevelt Library.
14. See telegrams from Walter White to Lowell Thomas, Gabriel Heater, Boake Carter, United Press, International News Service, Associated Press, and NAACP branches on October 27, 1934, in NAACP Papers, I, C-352.
15. Walter White to President Roosevelt, October 27, 1934, in NAACP Papers, I, C-352.

Homer Cummings, declaring, "Lynching today in Florida where event was advertised twelve hours in advance proves Federal government must act to check mobs. . . . We urge you to ask Congress for anti-lynching legislation as you did for special crime laws last session."[16] By October 31, White had secured promises from Senators Costigan and Wagner that they would reintroduce their bill in the next session. He also had resolved to dedicate the entire January, 1935, issue of *Crisis*, the NAACP magazine, to the topic of lynching and had secured the services of a dedicated, young, white social reformer, Howard "Buck" Kester, to investigate the particulars of the Neal lynching.[17] When Kester supplied White with a factual description, only ten days later, White believed that he had at last found the issue to stir the conscience of the nation.

The quickest and most dramatic way to keep the spotlight on the lynching issue would have been for Attorney General Cummings to move against the men responsible for Neal's murder. The two leading antilynching organizations in the South, the Commission on Interracial Cooperation and the Association of Southern Women for the Prevention of Lynching, sent telegrams to Cummings and to President Roosevelt on October 27 recommending that they invoke federal statutes for prohibiting kidnapping across a state boundary. Cummings rendered an immediate and, one must assume, precipitant reply to these telegrams, published in newspapers the following day. He declared that the Department of Justice had no authority to act in the Neal case under the Kidnapping Act, popularly known as the Lindbergh Act, because there was no question of ransom or reward involved in the case.[18]

White, perhaps on the advice of his close friend Charles Houston, dean of the Law School at Howard University, challenged the attorney general's position in a letter on October 29:

16. Walter White to Attorney General Homer Cummings, October 30, 1934, in NAACP Papers, I, C-352.
17. Walter White to Howard A. Kester, October 30, 1934, in NAACP Papers, I, C-352.
18. New York *Times*, October 28, 1934, p. 1.

We respectfully direct your attention to Section 408a of the United States Criminal Code (June 22, 1932, c. 271) (47 Stat. 326 as amended May 18, 1934, c. 301 48 Stat. 781), in which it is provided that "whoever shall knowingly transport or cause to be transported, or aid or abet in transporting, in interstate or foreign commerce, any person who shall have been unlawfully seized . . . or carried away by any means whatsoever and held for ransom or reward *or otherwise*" . . . shall, upon conviction be punished by death provided that the kidnapped person, "prior to the imposition of the penalty shall not have been liberated unharmed. . . ."

The italicized words, "or otherwise," in Section 408a would seem to us clearly to establish the authority of your department to proceed vigorously and promptly to apprehend and punish the lynchers of Neal. We respectfully urge that this be done.[19]

The secretary of the NAACP buttressed his view with a declaration of the bill's sponsor, Senator Royal S. Copeland, that his intent was to cover all kinds of kidnappings, hence inclusive of the Neal case.[20] In addition, White asked the opinions of America's leading legal authorities, hoping perhaps to use them, if helpful, in another letter to Cummings. The key words in the kidnapping statute were *or otherwise*. Were they to be loosely or strictly interpreted? The critical maneuver for White was to apply sufficient pressure on the attorney general to change his literal reading of the law. White and his friends were unable to muster this type of strength. Many ranking lawyers who were consulted agreed with White's position but with reservations. Edwin Borchard from Yale Law School warned that the attorney general "might feel that the Lindbergh Law was passed not for the purpose of punishing lynching, but for the purpose of punishing and preventing kidnaping . . . and that the seizure of Neal does not come under the heading of kidnaping." Professor K. N. Llewellyn of Columbia Law School wrote White, "I think the act as amended will bear your interpretation." Only Morris Ernst, from a prestigious New York law firm, believed that *or otherwise*

19. Walter White to Attorney General Homer S. Cummings, October 29, 1934, in NAACP Papers, I, C-352.

20. Royal S. Copeland to Walter White, November 2, 1934, in NAACP Papers, I, C-352.

"clearly indicated that the statute was no longer limited to cases of ransom or reward." Roscoe Pound from Harvard Law School, who wrote White he was "somewhat disappointed in coming to ... [his] conclusion," was "afraid" the *or otherwise* meant merely an advantage similar to ransom or reward and was not intended to introduce a series of new categories to prosecute such as lynching. He feared also that it was a "settled rule of interpretation" to give a "strict construction to penal statutes."[21]

Homer S. Cummings, attorney general of the United States, was an old-time Progressive who espoused FDR's "encore for reform" in the early 1930s. He had made a seconding speech nominating Roosevelt in 1932 at Chicago and was on intimate terms with the president.[22] Cummings shared the New Deal's philosophy that centralization of authority in the federal government was necessary to cope with the complexities of America's modern economy and technology. As attorney general he distinguished himself by expanding the powers of the FBI through proposing and helping to secure passage of legislation dealing with kidnapping, bank robbery, extortion, and racketeering. These laws gave the federal government authority in areas heretofore reserved for the states. Cummings' rationale was that modern crime, abetted by new facilities for transportation and communication, had become an organized, interstate operation which required federal jurisdiction. To break down resistance to federal intervention in the states, Cummings wished to avoid sweeping changes in the laws.[23] In fact, Cummings' policies were typical of Roosevelt's administration; he sought to work for the greater

21. Edwin M. Borchard to Walter White, November 10, 1934, K. N. Llewellyn to Walter White, November 2, 1934, Morris L. Ernst to Walter White, November 1, 1934, and Roscoe Pound to Walter White, November 5, 1934, all in NAACP Papers, I, C-352.

22. See Carl B. Swisher (ed.), *Selected Papers of Homer Cummings, Attorney General of the United States, 1933–1939* (New York: Scribner's, 1939). Most of Cummings' papers are at the University of Virginia, Charlottesville. A microfilm copy of the papers is at the Franklin D. Roosevelt Library. A great many of Cummings' letters are among the Franklin Roosevelt Papers.

23. Cummings' address at the "Attorney General's Conference on Crime" is located in Official File no. 10 of the Justice Department, November–December, 1934, National Archives.

good through a series of compromises with the states and other interest groups and to leave to the states authority over particular issues which fell outside general objectives.

Although Walter White would score Cummings and the Justice Department "a 100 percent performance in . . . the evasion of cases involving lynchings," his assumption that Cummings was merely "pulling a trick in getting around the Lindbergh Kidnaping Law" underestimated the complex motivation inspiring the attorney general.[24] Cummings was determined to put a comprehensive federal law enforcement program through the Congress. While pioneering a new relationship between the states and the federal government, Cummings would not risk collision with the southern bloc over a dubious issue which the Congress itself had not explicitly decided on.

On October 29, the assistant solicitor general, Angus D. MacLean, advised J. Edgar Hoover that the FBI should not enter the Neal case and corroborated Cummings' initial reaction to the Neal lynching.[25] Cummings remained steadfast in his interpretation as well. He wished to avoid "questions which might be embarrassing in connection with our general anti-crime program."[26]

The most complete statement of the attorney general's intent in the disposition of the Neal case actually came in 1935 when a black, Ab Young, was lynched in Mississippi after having fled to Tennessee where he was pursued and captured by a lynch mob. The attorney general in a memorandum to President Roosevelt referred to the legal circumstances of the Young and Neal cases

24. Walter White to George Soule, November 20, 1934, in NAACP Papers, I, C-106, reel 30; Walter White to Jessie D. Ames, November 6, 1934, in NAACP Papers, I, C-352.

25. The only copy of this memorandum was found in an FBI file on the Claude Neal case. See Angus D. McLean to Homer S. Cummings, Memorandum for the Attorney General, Re: Claude Neal-Lindbergh Law, October 29, 1934, in Files of the Federal Bureau of Investigation, no. 158260-58, Justice Department. FBI Director Hoover petitioned the attorney general for advice on the role of the FBI in cases like Neal's. He informed Cummings that the FBI had taken no investigative role in the Neal case. See J. Edgar Hoover to Attorney General Homer Cummings, October 30, 1934, in Files of the Federal Bureau of Investigation, no. 7-1157-2, Justice Department.

26. Swisher (ed.), *Papers of Homer Cummings*, 30.

as identical. He repeated again his conviction that the words *or otherwise* in the Kidnapping Act were not intended for sweeping application, rather when "particular words of description (i.e. ransom or reward) are followed by general terms (or otherwise) the latter will be regarded as referring to things of a like class." Cummings acknowledged the "criticism and pressure coming from various groups who for years, have been trying to get the Federal Government to deal with the crime of lynching." He believed that their insistence was motivated by a "justifiable hatred for the crime of lynching" but declared "it would seem to be rather doubtful policy to attempt . . . except upon a clear mandate from Congress."[27]

White did not forgive Cummings for his decision about Claude Neal's lynching as his satirical letter to Cummings on January 5, 1937, demonstrated. White wrote:

My dear Mr. Attorney General:
    We have read with interest the Associated Press dispatch of December 21 that you ordered the Bureau of Investigation of the Department of Justice to find a cloak which Mrs. Campbell Pritchett lost at a party given by you and Mrs. Cummings.
    Has the Bureau found Mrs. Pritchett's cloak yet? If so, may we inquire if it would be possible for you to assign the operatives thus freed by completion of that job to investigate the interstate kidnaping and subsequent lynching of Claude Neal in October, 1934, which, you may recall, we have been urging for more than two years.[28]

While Walter White engaged in a feud with the attorney general, he pursued a different course with the president and Mrs. Roosevelt. The NAACP secretary eagerly courted both to pressure Cummings to investigate the Jackson County incident and to win their support for the Wagner-Costigan antilynching bill,

27. Homer S. Cummings to President Franklin D. Roosevelt, March 20, 1935, in Presidential Papers, Official File 1489, Roosevelt Library. Cummings responded to a memo from President Roosevelt in which the latter wrote, "I am inclined to think Walter White is right. If his statement is correct, this man Abe [sic] Young was kidnapped. Please let me have your slant." Franklin D. Roosevelt to Homer S. Cummings, March 13, 1935, in Presidential Papers, President's Public File 1971, Roosevelt Library.
28. Walter White to Honorable Homer S. Cummings, January 5, 1937, in NAACP Papers, I, C-352.

which White believed had a chance for passage in the upcoming Seventy-fourth Congress.

White's campaign to enlist the official support of the president came, however, at an unfortunate time. The First Hundred Days of New Deal unanimity had passed. Recovery seemed halting; the country still was floundering in late 1934 with a depressed economy in which many millions were unemployed. While the president interpreted the solid liberal vote in the congressional elections in November, 1934, as a mandate to move the country farther to the left, he worried that his liberal program would produce a reaction among traditionalists and that a disaffected coalition of Republicans and southern Democrats might then hamstring necessary legislation. Although President Roosevelt abhorred lynching and personally endorsed antilynching legislation, he would table his concern for the issue. The country's needs for broad social legislation took precedence.

Roosevelt would obtain essential and critical legislation in the first session of Congress in 1935, including the Emergency Relief Appropriation Act launching the WPA, the Rural Electrification Administration, the National Youth Administration, the National Labor Relations Act guaranteeing the rights of unions to organize independently, the Public Utilities Holding Company Act, and the Social Security Act. This "Second Hundred Days" was probably the high-water mark of his personal success with Congress since its enactments were achieved at a time when Congress was beginning to exert genuine independence, unlike during the First Hundred Days. In order to obtain changes of this magnitude Roosevelt felt obliged to orchestrate divergent viewpoints and to avoid offending individual groups which comprised the essential majority.

Walter White communicated with Mrs. Roosevelt eleven times during the months of November and December, 1934, either about the Neal lynching or the impending Wagner-Costigan Bill.[29] Mrs. Roosevelt proved solicitous toward White's inquiries

29. The dates of these communications were November 8, 13, 20, and 27, and December 3, 11, 14, 15, 19, 20, and 27. See NAACP Papers, I, C-78, reel 12.

and requests, especially as an intermediary with the president. White wrote or wired FDR only twice during the same period.[30] By way of contrast, he received from the president gracious but noncommittal replies. On November 8, White expressed disappointment to Mrs. Roosevelt that Attorney General Cummings had not prosecuted Neal's lynchers and explained to her a growing skepticism, especially among Negroes, regarding the attitudes of the administration toward lynching. He asked her whether she or the president would make a public statement denouncing lynching. She conveyed the message to the president, adding her personal inscription, "I would like to, but will do whatever you say." A return note from the president's secretary Miss LeHand warned, "Pres. says this is dynamite." This led Mrs. Roosevelt to reply to White, "I do not feel it wise to speak on pending legislation, but I will talk to the President and see what can be done in some other way on this." Before receiving this letter, White had sent still another letter to Mrs. Roosevelt enclosing a mimeographed copy of the Kester report. He added, "I have investigated some forty-one lynchings and eight race riots and thought that I was almost immune to these tortures but this case has made me more ill and disheartened than any . . . which have occurred within my memory." She answered, "I talked with the President yesterday about your letter and he said that he hoped very much to get the Costigan-Wagner Bill passed in this coming session. The Marianna lynching was a horrible thing." And in response to White's request that Cummings prosecute the lynch mob which kidnapped Neal, she declared, "I wish very much that the Department of Justice might come to a different point of view and I think possibly they will."[31]

When White sought President Roosevelt's endorsement for the Wagner-Costigan Bill during the early weeks of the new session, he was stymied, even with Mrs. Roosevelt's assistance. She

30. NAACP Papers, I, C-73, reel 8.
31. Walter White to Eleanor Roosevelt, November 8, 1934, Eleanor Roosevelt to Walter White, November 20, 1934, Walter White to Eleanor Roosevelt, November 20, 1934, and Eleanor Roosevelt to Walter White, November 23, 1934, all in Eleanor Roosevelt Papers, Series 100, 1325, Roosevelt Library.

merely reassured White on January 8, 1935, that her husband would, "take up the subject . . . in his next conference with the leaders" but the NAACP secretary could get no promise of a follow-through. White could extract from him, at best, only an evasive statement; thus Mrs. Roosevelt wrote White, "His sentence on crime in his address to Congress touched on that because lynching is a crime."[32]

The NAACP leader would later turn to the president and Mrs. Roosevelt for last-minute personal intervention when a filibuster threatened passage of the Wagner-Costigan Bill. He concentrated most of his energy, however, on obtaining funds for the NAACP's drive for a federal antilynching law and gaining support for the measure from important persons.[33]

White recognized the potential shock value of the Neal lynching to secure his objectives. On October 30, just three days after Neal's death, he wired Kester in Nashville, Tennessee, and asked him to undertake the assignment on salary from the NAACP. When Kester agreed, White instructed him:

> We would like to get all the gruesome details possible together with any photographs of the body, crowd, etc. and as much evidence as is possible as to the identity of the leaders and members of the mob.
>   As the capacity of the American people for indignation is great, but short lived, get the facts to us as soon as possible.[34]

Buck Kester was well equipped to do a good job as an investigator for the NAACP. White had described him to a lawyer friend as "a first-rate young white man, who is absolutely right on the race question."[35] Kester, then in his early thirties, was a stocky, courageous rebel who already had become a legend among southern liberals and radicals.[36] In the 1920s he had organized the first

32. Eleanor Roosevelt to Walter White, January 8, 1935, and January 22, 1935, both in Eleanor Roosevelt Papers, Series 100, 1325, Roosevelt Library.

33. Walter White to William Rosenwald, November 16, 1934, in NAACP Papers, I, C-78, reel 12.

34. Walter White to Howard Kester, October 31, 1934, in NAACP Papers, I, C-78, reel 12.

35. Walter White to Leon Ransom, November 1, 1934, in NAACP Papers, I, C-78, reel 12.

36. See Edward M. Wayland (ed.), *The Papers of Howard Kester*, (14 reels on microfilm; Glen Rock, N.J.: Microfilming Corporation of America, 1973). The

student interracial group in the South. After a brief period at Princeton Theological Seminary, he returned to the South as secretary of the student YMCA at Vanderbilt. He lost his job for organizing a student protest against imperialism in China and became southern secretary of a liberal, internationalist organization—the Fellowship of Reconciliation. By the time of his assignment for the NAACP, Kester had received a divinity degree at Vanderbilt, preached the Social Gospel a short while, run for Congress on the Socialist ticket, and developed a reputation among black leaders for an absence of racial bias. He had won the last accolade by virtue of a summer spent under the tutelage of George Washington Carver at Tuskegee, a decision which had caused Kester's father to ask his son never to come home again.

On his way from Nashville to Marianna, Buck Kester detoured to Tuskegee to brief Dr. Carver on his mission. The two had been friends since 1926 when Carver was invited to speak at a YMCA summer institute in North Carolina, near Asheville. When Kester learned that no provision had been made for overnight accommodations or meals for the famous black scientist, he offered his own cabin to Dr. Carver and arranged a special room where interested white students were able to share dining facilities with him. Carver may have heard some of the details of the Neal lynching before Kester arrived. These were circulating among blacks at considerable distances from Marianna. Dr. Carver was apparently convinced that Kester's life was endangered in Jackson County and that the men who killed Neal might employ the same kinds of torture on him. He gave Kester a cyanide pellet with which to destroy himself quickly if he were captured and subjected to torture. He also gave Kester a chain to carry the pellet around his neck during his mission in Jackson County.[37]

Kester reached Marianna on Saturday, November 3. En route,

---

description of Kester used here is taken from lengthy correspondence to the author from H. L. Mitchell, his closest friend, who became with Buck Kester a cofounder of the historic Southern Tenant Farmers' Union. See H. L. Mitchell to author, December 10, 1977. See also, for mention of Kester's life at this time, Donald H. Grubbs, *Cry From the Cotton: The Southern Tenant Farmers' Union and the New Deal* (Chapel Hill: University of North Carolina Press, 1971).

37. H. L. Mitchell to author, December 10, 1977.

he wrote White, "I shall do my best to give you a finished job. I have my kodak with me." Marianna residents were unaccustomed to persons stopping over in their town for a week at a time, especially when their prime interest was to pry into details which had brought notoriety to the community. Kester apparently had a few white friends in the area who may have advised him how to gather information. He read back issues of a local newspaper and held conversations with persons who were either in the lynch mob or privy to its secrets as well as participants in the crowd at the Cannidy farm.[38] Kester's experience in Marianna was exhausting and nerve-shattering. On November 13 he described the effects of his week in Jackson County. "Scarcely have I ever had a more devastating experience than that. The lynching and subsequent developments are among the most ghastly things in the long history of lynching. My nerves were frayed. I was warned to get out of town before it was too late. I have not yet shaken the horror of the thing\off my mind. I was physically tired to death and my spirits were never at a lower ebb."[39]

Kester's report, originally sixteen mimeographed pages, is a classic journalistic account of the Neal lynching, its causes, and its aftermath.[40] As Walter White observed when introducing the report for a slick-back version which the NAACP distributed nationally, "This report is published with the hope that its sheer sadism and abnormal cruelty may stir thoughtful Americans to action. If this report does not do so we fear the situation is hopeless."[41] Indeed, it is difficult to forget Kester's description of "the little children, some of them mere tots who . . . waited with sharpened sticks for the return of Neal's body," or by implication, the parents who encouraged them to do so. Kester also wrote,

38. Howard Kester to Walter White, November 1, 1934, in NAACP Papers, I, C-352; Howard A. Kester, "The Marianna, Florida Lynching," 1–17, in Lynching File, Series 278, Florida State Archives.

39. Howard Kester to C. C., November 18, 1934, in Wayland (ed.), *Papers of Howard Kester*, reel 1.

40. For the original mimeograph report see "The Marianna, Florida Lynching" in NAACP Papers, I, C-352.

41. National Association for the Advancement of Colored People, *The Lynching of Claude Neal* (New York: n.p., 1934), 1, copy in Lynching File, Series 278, Florida State Archives.

"Fingers and toes from Neal's body have been exhibited as sou-
venirs in Marianna where one man offered to divide the finger
which he had with a friend as 'a special favor'." Another man had
"one of the fingers preserved in alcohol"; photographs of Neal's
body were difficult to get because "those who had them would
not part with them. I offered from 50¢ to $5.00 for one." Kester
also summed up the horrors of the Marianna riots, quoting a man
whose wife shielded her maid from the mob as saying, "Saturday
was a day of terror and madness . . . never to be forgotten by anyone." [42]

White was convinced that Kester had provided the NAACP
with its best piece of propaganda to fight lynching. He wrote Joel
Springarn of the NAACP, "We are leaving no stone unturned in
our effort to raise sufficient funds to enable us to make the distri-
bution nationwide." One needs only to inspect the vast bulk of
materials on the Neal case in the NAACP files of the Library of
Congress and compare them with the much smaller collections
for other lynching cases to realize the magnitude of the NAACP's
commitment. The entire first printing of five thousand copies of
the Kester report was exhausted six days after delivery. Ten thousand additional copies were ordered, and White made plans to
publish a hundred thousand copies. [43] Many were given away to
businessmen, congressmen, ministers, and newspaper editors.
Copies of the report appeared verbatim in a Mexico City daily
and a French magazine. [44] Hundreds of requests to purchase copies
came to NAACP offices from all over the country. [45] Most reactions showed that White had correctly predicted its shocking effects. Kelly Miller, the distinguished black sociologist at Howard,

42. Howard Kester to Walter White, November 13, 1934, in NAACP Papers, I,
C-352; NAACP, *The Lynching of Claude Neal*, 2.
43. Walter White to Joel Springarn, December 22, 1934, in NAACP Papers, I,
C-154; Walter White to Mrs. L. Posener, December 14, 1934, and memorandum
from Walter White to Roy Wilkins, December 17, 1934, both in NAACP Papers, I,
C-352.
44. The Kester report was reprinted verbatim in *El Nacional*, December 25,
1934, p. 1, and in *Les Cahiers Des Droits de L'homme*, February 20, 1935, p. 1.
Copies are in NAACP Papers, I, C-352.
45. There were over three hundred individual requests in NAACP Papers, I,
C-352.

remarked on receipt of the report, "This was a masterpiece of work and will do much to open the eyes of the country." Other readers also expressed themselves. A businessman wrote White, "The report on the Neal lynching you sent me almost made me ill, and the unavoidable contemplation of it has tormented me ever since." "I am numb with sorrow and shame," wrote another who now resolved to make her usual contribution to NAACP despite financial difficulties. A unique response came from Henry L. Mencken. Sensing a superb opportunity to harpoon the whole civilization, he purchased several copies and sent them to his Christian friends with an attached Christmas card. Mencken declared, "Somehow it seemed to me a nifty idea."[46]

With outrage over the Neal case fresh in the minds of many influential Americans, White intensified his campaign against lynching with the convening of the Seventy-fourth Congress. He repeatedly sought an appointment with President Roosevelt in December just before its opening session. He had hoped to personally present the president with a memorial denouncing lynching signed by a blue-ribbon group of American citizens which included 9 governors, 27 mayors, 58 bishops and churchmen, 54 university and college presidents, and 109 lawyers, publishers, editors, and writers.[47] Roosevelt did not respond immediately to White's request, presumably because such a meeting might be construed as public endorsement of the Wagner-Costigan Bill. He relied on Marvin McIntyre's opinion of whether to meet White. On December 26, he wrote in a "Memo to Mac," "What do you think of this [question by White]? In any event I could not see them Friday but I could see them the following week. If you arrange an appointment, will you tell Mrs. Roosevelt." McIntyre wired White, "Impossible arrange appointment until after opening of Congress. Will advise you then." No advice was forthcom-

46. Kelly Miller to Walter White, December 13, 1934, Henry C. Patterson to Walter White, December 10, 1934, and Mabel E. Simpson to Walter White, January 6, 1935, all in NAACP Papers, I, C-154; H. L. Mencken to Walter White, December 26, 1934, in NAACP Papers, I, C-352.
47. The entire list is published in *Punishment for the Crime of Lynching: Hearing Before a Subcommittee of the Committee on the Judiciary, United States Senate,* 74th Cong., 1st Sess., on S. 24, February 14, 1935, pp. 33–38.

ing. The NAACP leader thereupon forwarded his memorial through the mail on December 27. He also sponsored interfaith rallies to denounce lynching, especially featuring speakers who called for effective federal legislation.[48]

White's most novel program to win popular support and funding for federal antilynching legislation was the Art Commentary on Lynching, an exhibit held at the Arthur U. Newton Galleries, 11 East Fifty-seventh Street, New York, from February 15 to March 2, 1935.[49] It was another of those projects in which White brought together the "best people" of both races. While he probably overestimated the impact of art afficianados on the outcome of legislation, the exhibit made for pleasant company and fulfilled other needs for interracial socializing.

The Neal episode and the Kester report were major, behind-the-scenes inspirations for the exhibit. White had appealed to both patrons and artists with appended copies of Kester's work. The exhibit was originally scheduled for the Jacques Seligmann Galleries, but four days before opening, NAACP officials learned that Seligmann had decided not to house the exhibit, apparently because of "political, economic, and social pressure." Arthur Newton read about the homeless exhibition and decided to accept it.

Nearly three thousand people trudged through severe winter weather to view the fifteen-day exhibit. Many of them probably read the forewords in the handsome exhibit catalogue written by Sherwood Anderson and Erskine Caldwell. Anderson took to task the idea that blacks were lynched to preserve the sexual purity of white women in the South. "Look at Scottsboro. Does anyone really believe that the white men, the poor whites who crowd into the court room down there . . . believe they are trying to protect the two white women in that affair? Poor whites in the South lynched blacks because that was the only thing left to

48. FDR to Marvin McIntyre, December 26, 1934, and Marvin McIntyre to Walter White, December 26, 1934, both in Presidential Papers, President's Public File 1336, Roosevelt Library; Memorandum from Walter White to ministers, January 5, 1935, in NAACP Papers, I, C-331.
49. Information on the Art Commentary on Lynching is derived principally from a copy of the catalogue for the exhibit located in Schomburg Research Center in New York, and from *Crisis*, XLII (April, 1935), 106.

them to achieve self-dignity." "It is then," he declared, "simply an assertion, ugly and perverted, of man's hunger for self-respect. I cannot get it from the factory where cheap goods are made. I must get it somewhere. Let me kill, kill, kill. At least that is an expression of physical might." Erskine Caldwell believed that education was the key to eliminating lynchings but called for federal legislation to help the South put its house in order.

The spectators viewed thirty-nine paintings, ten of which were by blacks. Among the better known paintings and lithographs exhibited were George Bellows' "The Law Is Too Slow," Julius Block's "Prisoner," Reginald Marsh's "This is Her First Lynching," and Jose Orozco's "Negroes." "This is Her First Lynching" showed a young white girl being held by her mother over the heads of the mob so the child could get a better view of the torture being inflicted on a black victim. The lesser known painters and their works included George Biddle's "Alabama Code: Our Girls Don't Sleep With Niggers," William Chase's "Son, derned if that nigger ain't made us late for the prayer meetin'," and Irwin Hoffman's "In Dixie Land I Take My Stand to Live and Die in Dixie."

Memories of Neal's fate hung like a postscript to the grim titles for each painting. For at least two painters his lynching provided direct inspiration. Allan Freelon, a young black painter, sent his "Barbecue—American Style" to the exhibit "to record the horror of what has come to be a major sports event with radio announcement and invitations in advance."[50] Harry Sternberg submitted "Southern Holiday," which portrayed a lynching with mutilation. The artist wrote a wry commentary to accompany his painting: "Pass by quickly, nice people; Retain your fixed smile. This is not something that happened only once, somewhere, when the maniac got loose."[51] Not many spectators who attended opening night lingered before the paintings. One observer recalled that the guests soon began to talk happily with one another, ignoring the paintings; and word quickly passed among the tender-hearted

50. Allan Freelon to Walter White, February 2, 1935, in NAACP Papers, I, C-206.
51. New York *Post*, February 18, 1935, clipping in NAACP Papers, I, C-352.

Fig. 10. Allan Freelon's "Barbeque—American Style," displayed at the Art Commentary on Lynching, February 15–March 2, 1935, in New York, in the aftermath of the Neal lynching.

From NAACP Papers, courtesy of National Association for the Advancement of Colored People.

that there were other, more pleasant exhibits elsewhere. Mrs. Roosevelt was given a personal invitation by White. She attended with reservation because of the political implication of her visit. She wrote Walter White:

> The more I think about going to the exhibition, the more troubled I am, so this morning I went in to talk to my husband about it and asked him what they really planned to do about the Bill because I was afraid that some bright newspaper reporter might write a story which would offend some of the southern members and thereby make it even more difficult to do anything about the Bill.
>
> My husband said it was quite all right for me to go, but if some reporter took the occasion to describe some horrible picture, it would cause more southern opposition. They plan to bring the Bill out quietly as soon as possible although two southern Senators have said they would filibuster for two weeks. He thinks, however, they can get it through.[52]

And she was troubled by what she saw, especially by the news that the NAACP secretary was preparing to send the exhibit on tour to southern cities after it closed in New York. One detects the president's concern for giving offense to the South in her letter to White of March 23, 1935.

> In thinking it over, I do not feel that with the exception of a few things, the exhibit had tremendous artistic value. I do realize all the advantages of having things put before people in a visual way, but think that we must be very careful where and how we do it. We do not want to start passions in the South which will make horrible occurrences any more frequent than they are, particularly when the Bill is being discussed and there will be enough speeches in Congress.[53]

The Art Commentary made it to only one other city, Baltimore, where it was also well received. Shortages in funds forced cancellation in seventeen other cities where it was tentatively scheduled. Reviews had been generally good. The New York *World Telegram* commented on February 18, 1935, "To any who hold that art cannot be propaganda and still be true and great art

---

52. Eleanor Roosevelt to Walter White, February, 1935, in Eleanor Roosevelt Papers, Series 100, 1325, Roosevelt Library.

53. Eleanor Roosevelt to Walter White, March 23, 1935, in NAACP Papers, I, C-73, reel 8.

we recommend a visit to the Arthur U. Newton Gallery." The critic added: "Remember this is not an exhibition for softies. It may upset your stomach. If it upsets your complacency on the subject it will have been successful."[54] As an exhibit of social realism, the Art Commentary on Lynching had few equals in its decade. The great discomfort the exhibit produced was perhaps the best sign that the days of public lynchings in the United States were numbered.

Walter White had engineered a magnificent campaign to get the facts to influential Americans and to lay the groundwork for a legislative victory. It now was a matter of getting Congress to act and if its members faltered then to enlist the president's support. He wrote letters to members of the Congress and supplied them with statistics and letters of endorsement from organizations purporting to represent more than forty million people. He also appeared before the Senate judiciary subcommittee in mid-February, 1935, and submitted the memorial to outlaw lynching and the Kester report for the record.[55]

On March 11, 1935, the Senate Judiciary Committee reported favorably on the Wagner-Costigan antilynching bill and the measure went on the Senate calendar. White wrote a friend of NAACP, "We have reason to feel confident that *if a vote is secured* the bill will pass both houses of Congress. President Roosevelt has assured me personally that he would gladly sign the bill." By April, 43 senators and 123 congressmen had declared their support for Wagner-Costigan, some of them acknowledging that the lynching in Jackson County had made them more determined than ever to endorse federal antilynching legislation.[56] White expected additional pledges from other members of Congress.

As a seasoned lobbyist, White was under no illusions about the

54. *Crisis*, XLII (April, 1935), 106.
55. *Punishment for the Crime of Lynching: Hearing Before a Subcommittee of the Committee on the Judiciary, United States Senate*, 74th Cong., 1st Sess., on S. 24, February 14, 1935.
56. Walter White to "Friend," March 13, 1935, in NAACP Papers, I, C-78; Walter White to Mrs. Eleanor Roosevelt, April 10, 1935, in Eleanor Roosevelt Papers, Series 100, 1362, Roosevelt Library.

intransigent opposition to be expected from the southern bloc. After having maneuvered through lesser obstacles on his own, he turned to the first family for aid against the anticipated filibuster. On April 10, before the Wagner-Costigan Bill was introduced to the Senate for debate, he wrote Mrs. Roosevelt:

> Indications from all parts of the country seem to establish that the country at large would not stand for a filibuster against the bill, providing a sufficiently determined stand against the filibuster were made. Unfortunately, there is a very widespread and rapidly growing cynicism on the part of many colored and white people as to whether or not the anti-lynching bill will really be voted on at this session. I need hardly add that I do not share this doubt.[57]

White could not have been requesting the president's favor at a worse time. Roosevelt's major legislative proposals affecting the economic well-being and social welfare of the country were still pending. Senator Costigan himself acknowledged that his bill did not compare in importance with the legislative priorities on the president's agenda. He wrote Roosevelt on April 22, "The New York *Times* this morning reports that 'Southern Senators will filibuster against the anti-lynching bill, and your legislative program will be halted.' Needless to say, I have no wish to obstruct your legislative proposals of major importance." White's hopes persisted, however. He kept Mrs. Roosevelt informed on the tally of senators for and against the bill as it reached the Senate floor on April 24, adding a muted request for help, "I can be reached during the day at Senator Costigan's office."[58]

White's message of April 24 to Mrs. Roosevelt was probably written after he had spent the day in the Senate chamber observing angry southern senators writhe as Costigan attempted merely to explain his bill. No one knew how many senators would vote with Wagner and Costigan. A simple way to find out was to vote for adjournment of the session. Senator Joe Robinson of Arkan-

---

57. Walter White to Eleanor Roosevelt, April 10, 1935, in Eleanor Roosevelt Papers, Series 100, 1362, Roosevelt Library.

58. Senator Edward Costigan to President Franklin D. Roosevelt, April 22, 1935, in Presidential Papers, Official File 1489, Roosevelt Library; Walter White to Eleanor Roosevelt, April 24, 1934, in Eleanor Roosevelt Papers, Series 100, 1362, Roosevelt Library.

sas, the majority leader, who stood shoulder to shoulder with his colleagues from the South on this issue, did so move. Adjournment might have placed the measure in limbo. But his proposal was defeated, 34 to 33, and that slim majority then held to vote recess instead.[59] Recess merely deferred the legislative day and hence assured that the bill would continue on the active business of the chamber.

White had seen enough; it was a close call. He wired the president and asked for an immediate appointment and warned: "It is now apparent that only word from you to the Senate or the country at large will break filibuster and insure vote on this bill. . . . Made several unsuccessful efforts to obtain appointment with you yesterday to place before you seriousness of the situation."[60] But the NAACP secretary knew where to locate the keys to the president's conscience. White phoned Mrs. Roosevelt, and she invited him to a Sunday afternoon conference at the White House.

The president arrived while White was talking with the president's wife and his mother on the porch of the White House. It was a bright spring afternoon. Roosevelt had been cruising on the Potomac and was late for the meeting. He began the conversation with typical exuberance and storytelling, and it was only with difficulty that White was able to get the conversation around to antilynching legislation. Roosevelt was forced finally to tell White that southerners chaired key congressional committees: "If I come out for the anti-lynching bill now, they will block every bill I ask Congress to pass to keep America from collapsing. I just can't take that risk."[61]

One can only speculate about White's feelings as he left the White House. It had been a magnificent campaign which had kept the needs of blacks before the country at a time when injustices to them had been submerged in the broader issue of economic recovery. Clearly, he did not despair. Perhaps the best in-

59. *Congressional Record*, 74th Cong., 1st Sess., 6369.
60. Walter White to Franklin D. Roosevelt, April 26, 1935, in Presidential Papers, Official File 93-A, Roosevelt Library.
61. Walter White, *A Man Called White: The Autobiography of Walter White* (New York: Viking, 1948), 168–70.

sight into his thought came seven months later when White would submit to the president "a statement of issues which are of greatest concern to American Negroes and concerning which they are most anxious."[62] Lynchings topped the list, even before discrimination in relief and public works and civil service, the white primaries, and discrimination in the armed forces.

The filibuster continued in the Senate chamber through May 1, a total of six days. Hugo Black, James Byrnes, John H. Bankhead, and Cotton Ed Smith all figured in the endless speechmaking. Costigan gave up hope for immediate action on his proposal. He informed Roosevelt on April 26, after the filibuster began, that he and Wagner would put aside their antilynching bill "in view of the expected close vote" in order for the Senate to act on NRA, AAA amendments, Social Security, and other measures of "your 'must program'." Roosevelt made a final public statement on the bill before the Seventy-fourth Congress in reply to Costigan on May 1, 1935. He compromised once more and gave support to both camps simultaneously in declaring, "As you know I have been wholly in favor of decent discussion."[63] When Robinson made his motion to adjourn, his fourth since the bill was introduced, his leadership was accepted on the afternoon of May 1 by 48 to 32.

White kept fighting, but the most opportune time in the 1930s had passed when the Wagner-Costigan antilynching bill failed in 1935. Familiar patterns unfolded in late 1935 and 1936, when legislation was dictated by election-year considerations, and in 1937 and 1938 when the congressional alliance against administration programs had virtually neutralized the New Deal and Roosevelt needed support from southern congressmen even more than before. Mrs. Roosevelt continued to plead for Walter White in the White House, and she also wrote him optimistic letters, but the

62. Memorandum from Walter White to Franklin D. Roosevelt, January 2, 1936, in Presidential Papers, Official File 93-A, Roosevelt Library.

63. Edward Costigan to Franklin Roosevelt, April 26, 1935, and Franklin D. Roosevelt to Edward P. Costigan, May 1, 1935, both in Presidential Papers, President's Public File 1971, Roosevelt Library.

southern bloc remained unmoved and the president was unwilling to bring pressure against them.[64]

While the official reaction to the Neal affair did not go as far as Walter White had wished, there were unmistakable signs that the end of public-style lynchings was imminent and that Claude Neal's death had helped sensitize public opinion to that effect. No presidential family had shown such an interest in the subject previously. Antilynching bills made it to the floor of both houses of Congress twice within three years (in 1935 and 1937), again an unprecedented achievement.[65] The NAACP had never expended such effort previously nor marshaled such publicity in its drive for antilynching reform, and it had never before commanded the allegiance of so many Americans. The national conscience, so long dormant on lynching, had at last begun to stir in the 1930s.

64. Eleanor Roosevelt to Walter White, March 19, 1936, in Eleanor Roosevelt Papers, Series 100, 1411, Roosevelt Library.
65. For additional discussion of efforts to pass an antilynching bill in 1930s, see Jesse Reeder, "Federal Efforts to Control Lynching" (M.A. thesis, Cornell University, 1952), 90–98.

Chapter 7

The End of
an American
Tragedy

After 1935, the era of lynchings in the form of public murder of blacks with attendant rituals came rapidly to an end in America.[1] Whereas the number of official lynchings of blacks in 1933, 1934, and 1935 averaged nineteen each year, in only five years thereafter did the number exceed five, and for more than half those years only one black or none at all lost life in this fashion.[2] The traditional practice by this time had become repulsive to all but a small number of whites: the call to arms, the gathering of white men in the darkened courthouse square to give chase, the manhunt or seizure from jail, attribution of heroism and justice to those who avenged the community's good name, mutilation of the victim's body and display of his remains in a public spectacle, and the photographing of hanging corpses for the sake of remembrance. Although acts of terror against blacks in the South continued, most of them might better be described as murders, because of the small number of persons involved in their con-

1. Gunnar Myrdal, Richard Sterner and Arnold Rose, *An American Dilemma: The Negro Problem and Modern Democracy* (New York: Harper and Row, 1944), 565–66.

2. One of the best treatments of lynching in the late thirties and early forties is Jessie Daniel Ames, *The Changing Character of Lynching: Review of Lynching, 1931–1934* (Atlanta: n.p., 1942). The best statistics on lynchings are in *The Negro Almanac* (New York: Bellwether, 1971), 270, taken from the Tuskegee Institute Archives, Tuskegee, Alabama, which has complete records through 1968.

140

cealment, rather than as lynchings with their public participation and public rituals.[3] When one considers the long and intense practice of lynching blacks in the South and its attendant ceremonies, the rapid decline of the phenomenon and its disappearance from public view is striking.

There were, of course, regressions such as the grisly incident of a lynching by blowtorch in 1937 at Duck Hill, Mississippi.[4] Two young blacks accused of killing a country store operator were held in the town square while a mob of hundreds gathered to watch as mob leaders burned them with acetylene torches prior to hanging their bodies on nearby tree limbs. Another brutal event occurred in Monroe, Georgia, in 1946 when four of the six blacks lynched that year were put to death in that community.[5] But places like Duck Hill and Monroe were isolated pockets of traditionalism, remote from and impervious to nationalizing influences.

While it would be a mistake to argue that the Neal affair, by itself, produced the complex changeover, it would probably also be wrong to see Neal's death as simply another entry in the statistics of southern violence. This particular lynching tripped strong retaliatory forces in the national community. It demonstrated that modern technology—the news services, the photographs and films that could be taken, and the travel facilities that could be used by reporters and cameramen—had decisively removed the advantage of anonymity from those bent on mob action. The national community had both the resources to force its way into Jackson County for information and the prestige to coerce lynch-

3. *The Negro Almanac*, 268–70; Lynching Records, 1962–68, Tuskegee Institute Archives. On the changing character of lynchings, which now more closely resembled murders, see *Lynching Goes Underground* (n.p., n.d.), published anonymously about 1940 and available in Association of Southern Women for the Prevention of Lynching Papers, Trevor-Arnett Library, Atlanta University, Atlanta, Georgia. Examples of murders committed against blacks whose bodies were found in desolate places are the deaths of Emmet Till in August, 1955, in Money, Mississippi, and Mack John Parker on the Pearl River, also in Mississippi, in 1959. See Lynching Records, Boxes 55–57, Tuskegee Institute.

4. H. L. Mitchell to author, February 15, 1977. Mitchell was a close friend of Kester, who also investigated this incident for the NAACP.

5. New York *Times*, July 27, 1946, pp. 1, 6.

ers to stand trial before the court of public opinion for their misdeeds. While the absence of effective opposition within the local community had once encouraged lynching, the new national community created by the media now provided an effective inhibitor. Newspaper coverage and editorial criticism of the Neal lynching may well have been the most complete for any lynching of a black in American history. Surely, NAACP files contain many more newspaper clippings and headlines about Neal's death than any other lynching of a black.[6] This explains why the editor of the Jackson County *Floridan* found it necessary to justify the action taken against Neal as his locale came under attack by the national press and why Mayor Burton, who sought the economic development of Marianna, was forced to implore Pathe News not to show films of the riot. Outside pressures had developed such a fear of embarrassment over exposure that Jackson County and similar areas, where there were still many people who believed in the mob tradition, complied, outwardly at least, with national norms. An editorial writer for the Richmond *Times-Dispatch* who endorsed a federal antilynching bill in 1937 perceived the issue clearly when he declared the newspaper's support for legislation "to put a stop to the seemingly endless series of murders which have disgraced the South and America before the world."[7] To continue the practice meant to forfeit one's place in a world which had become increasingly sensitive to moral issues such as lynching.

State officials in Florida, stung by the avalanche of letters protesting the inhumanity of the Neal lynching when they hoped to promote Florida's tourism and economic future, also were chagrined, especially the self-styled progressive governor, David Sholtz. When another lynching seemed likely in Levy County, Florida, in March, 1935, and a representative of the Association of Southern Women for the Prevention of Lynching wired him "to prevent another Marianna," Governor Sholtz replied, "I do

6. National Association for the Advancement of Colored People (NAACP) Papers, Manuscript Division, Library of Congress.
7. Jackson County *Floridan*, November 8, 1934, p. 4; Richmond *Times-Dispatch*, February 2, 1937, p. 6

appreciate the circumstances that developed in the Marianna lynching and nothing has been left undone to avoid a repetition of that occurrence."[8] But Sholtz's successor, Fred P. Cone, affectionately known as "Old Suwanee" was a throwback to the old days. His temperament is suggested by a memorable statement made on the occasion of his trip to New York in 1937: "I think a man ought to be hung on a tree if he advocates overthrow of the government."[9] He seemed to have upgraded lynching from a species of racism to a question of patriotism. Despite his conservative mentality and a temporary resurgence of lynching in Florida during his administration, residents of the state are credited with thwarting almost twice as many intended lynchings.

The growing sensitivity among southerners to the moral evil of public lynchings also deterred those who wished to perform them. Though this phenomenon was gradual in the twentieth-century South as that region became more modern and urban, by the mid-1930s would-be lynchers were experiencing increasing disfavor throughout the South. Here too the lynching of Neal had a catalytic effect. Noting the upsurge of editorial condemnation of lynching and support for a federal antilynching law in fifteen southern newspapers including the prestigious Birmingham *News-Age-Herald*, Louisville *Courier-Journal*, and Richmond *Times-Dispatch*, Virginius Dabney, writing in *The Nation* in 1937, ascribed major importance to the impact of the Neal episode: "An incident which must have had enormous influence in swinging many citizens of Dixie over to the view that the time has come to stop playing around the fringes of the lynching problem was the sickening killing of Claude Neal."[10] The "Neal Affair," Dabney declared, was disillusioning for intelligent southerners because it provided "convincing evidence to unbiased minds that some Southern states were wholly unwilling to pro-

8. Telegram from Mrs. William P. Cornell (Chairman of Florida Council of Association of Southern Women for the Prevention of Lynching) to Governor David Sholtz, March 21, 1935, and David Sholtz to Mrs. W. P. Cornell, April 12, 1935, both in Lynching File, Series 278, Florida State Archives, Tallahassee.

9. New York *Times*, October 22, 1937, p. 23.

10. Virginius Dabney, "Dixie Rejects Lynching," *Nation*, CVL (November 27, 1937), 581.

ceed against lynchers." Dabney believed that a sufficient number
of southerners were so "disgusted over the situation," primarily
due to the Neal lynching and the "blow-torch barbarity at Duck
Hill, Mississippi" that they had become convinced the answer
was a federal law. It is also interesting to note that the South's
best organized foe of lynching, the Commission on Interracial
Cooperation, endorsed a federal bill for the first time in 1935 and
that the Association of Southern Women for the Prevention of
Lynching had first become an effective organization in that year,
with thirty-five thousand members. Indeed, for the first time a
majority of southerners supported legislation making lynching a
federal crime, according to the findings of a Gallup Poll.[11]

Along with perceptible changes in public opinion in the South,
the weight of that opinion could be more effectively exercised
even in increasingly remote areas with the emergence in several
southern states of efficient highway patrols employing radio
communication in their patrol vehicles. This technical innova-
tion deterred the gala lynching celebrations. Jessie Daniel Ames
credited the organization of efficient state patrols using radio
communication in six southern states in 1938 for reducing numbers of both lynchings and attempted lynchings.[12]

A third major retaliatory force which had an effect in deterring
mob violence toward blacks came from the federal government.
The New Deal's conscious intent to replace older individualism
with nationalizing controls was well demonstrated in its interest
in the lynching question. Although it passed no antilynching bill,
the support of the president and Mrs. Roosevelt, the appearance
of the two antilynching bills on the floor of both the House and
the Senate, and the capable leadership of Senator Robert Wagner
of New York had the effect of intimidating those who would
lynch blacks.[13] According to Walter White, lynchings declined at
times when it seemed passage of an antilynching bill was imminent.[14]

11. *The Gallup Poll* (New York: Random House, 1972), 48, 75.
12. Ames, *The Changing Character of Lynching*, 16.
13. Jesse W. Reeder, "Federal Efforts to Control Lynching" (M. A. thesis, Cornell University, 1952), 90–98.
14. See Walter White's remarks in *Punishment for the Crime of Lynching:*

Despite the fact that federal antilynching bills were success-fully filibustered or blocked during the Roosevelt and Truman administrations, both presidents pledged the moral weight of their office to end the abuse. After the successful filibuster staged by southern senators in 1938, Roosevelt declared that ways had to be found to curb all forms of mob violence, including labor troubles as well as lynchings. He suggested this could be done in two ways: "Have the Attorney General investigate all acts of mob violence, ascertain the facts and promptly make them pub-lic to the President, Congress and the press, or, if that were not satisfactory, have Congress set up a standing committee to deter-mine the facts and make them public." In the face of the congres-sional impasse, Roosevelt obviously sensed that exposure was the most effective cure for lynching. He called for "a full exposi-tion of the facts in incidents that occur in every part of the na-tion."[15]

Liberals in the Roosevelt camp also made new administrative weapons available to blacks; these established that the federal government had powers to punish lynchers even without an anti-lynching statute. As early as 1937 Walter White reported to col-leagues in the NAACP that a representative of the State Com-mittee Investigating Violations of Civil and Other Liberties "would stretch a point, if need be, in looking into some phase of the violation of civil liberties of Negroes." White then declared, "The Claude Neal [case] seems to me to be the best case to open up the whole question of the treatment of the Negro."[16] On Feb-ruary 3, 1939, Attorney General of the United States Frank Mur-phy established a Civil Liberties Unit, later called the Civil Rights Section, within the Criminal Division of the Department of Justice. The new organization was designed to study civil rights as provided by the Constitution and acts of Congress and

---

Hearing Before a Subcommittee of the Committee on the Judiciary, United States Senate, 74th Cong., 1st Sess., on S. 24, February 14, 1935, pp. 32–59, and Walter White to President Franklin D. Roosevelt, June 17, 1938, in Presidential Papers, President's Public File 1336, Franklin D. Roosevelt Library, Hyde Park, New York.

15. Atlanta *Constitution*, March 23, 1938, p. 4.

16. Walter White's memorandum to J. E. and A. B. Springarn, Charles H. Hous-ton, and Roy Wilkins, January 20, 1937, in NAACP Papers, C-352.

to conduct prosecutions against civil rights violators. The Civil Rights Section subsequently investigated complaints about lynchings to establish whether federal statutes had been violated and recommended passage of a federal antilynching law.[17]

As war with the fascist powers appeared imminent, President Roosevelt made further overtures to Walter White's preeminent concern for American blacks. Roosevelt appealed to the leadership of the NAACP to remain steadfast to America's ideals as he himself became more active in guaranteeing their realization through administrative fiat. In a letter to Walter White on June 13, 1939, he asked that White and the NAACP see themselves "as an integral group in our American democracy . . . to uphold its ideals, to help to carry its burdens and to partake of its blessings."[18] And to Arthur B. Springarn, president of the NAACP, he wrote in June, 1940:

> Democracy as a way of life faces today its most severe challenge. It is challenged by adversaries—men and women that deny full liberty to the individual. In the face of this challenge, the American democracy must marshal all its strength of its people in a unity of conviction and purpose. Such organizations as yours bear a full measure of responsibility in helping make this unity and this internal strength invulnerable.[19]

Roosevelt's wartime administration relating to blacks is chiefly remembered for his issuing an executive order in June, 1941, setting up the Fair Employment Practices Commission to create nondiscriminatory employment practices. But still another measure which met with favor with the NAACP was his directive in 1942 to the Department of Justice to make an automatic investigation of all cases of deaths of blacks in which there was any suspicion of lynching. At last, Walter White's anguished pleas

17. Henry A. Schweinhaut, "The Civil Liberties Section of the Department of Justice," *Bill of Rights Review*, I (1940–41), 206–207. See also attorney general's order no. 3204, February 3, 1939, quoted in Robert K. Carr, *Federal Protection of Civil Rights: Quest for a Sword* (Ithaca: Cornell University Press, 1947), 24–25.
18. Franklin D. Roosevelt to Walter White, June 13, 1939, in Presidential Papers, President's Public File 1336, Roosevelt Library.
19. Franklin D. Roosevelt to Arthur B. Springarn, June 14, 1940, in Presidential Papers, President's Public File 1336, Roosevelt Library.

over Claude Neal had been answered, although in actual practice the Justice Department investigated only a relatively small number of cases. President Truman, in response to an incensed public opinion over the wholesale lynchings in Monroe, Georgia, in 1946 appointed a special committee which called for a stiff federal antilynching statute including fines and prison terms for officials who failed to take proper steps to bring lynchers to justice. Truman also made vigorous pleas for an antilynching bill as did his attorney general, Tom Clark.[20]

It is ironic that the president who obtained successful passage of the nation's first effective federal antilynching bill came himself from an area of central Texas which was unsurpassed in its record of violence. While Lyndon Johnson's Vietnam policy may have been, as Richard M. Brown asserts, "a throw back to the central Texas ethic of violent self-defense," he took particular pride as a southerner in healing the nation's wounds between blacks and whites. The Civil Rights Act of 1968 outlawed acts of violence "by one or more persons, part of an assemblage of three or more persons which act or acts . . . shall result in . . . injury . . . to the person of any other individual." Violators were subject to fines of not more than ten thousand dollars or imprisonment for not more than five years or both.[21] By this time the remnant of southern opposition to federal antilynching bills in Congress was speechless. The scales had been tipped by modernization and urbanization as well as the logic of the war against the fascist powers and the Cold War against communism. The Warren court had made decisions in the 1950s which forced Americans to become conscious of deprivations in civil rights. During the 1960s the executive branch threw powerful support into the civil rights cause, and the news media flushed out pockets of bigotry with unblinking accuracy. Prosperity in the 1950s and 1960s was another firm ally of tolerance. And, of course, so were the blacks

20. Carr, *Federal Protection of Civil Rights*, 164; Reeder, "Federal Efforts to Control Lynching," 98–101.
21. Richard M. Brown, *Strain of Violence: Historical Studies of American Violence and Vigilantism* (New York: Oxford University Press, 1975), 238; *United States Statutes at Large*, 1968, LXXXII, 76.

themselves, since they were at last an effective political unit in the Democratic party where their interests were acknowledged.

The nation's assertion that it would no longer tolerate calculated murder based on race produced light years of progress in race relations. That ethic met with such wide approval that the artificial mores of insular areas could not withstand its force. Though clandestine violence against blacks continued in the South, the band no longer played for such people anywhere. They worked in smaller and smaller circles and retreated into history with quickening strides.

Chapter 8

Conclusion

What can democracy ultimately mean except respect for the lives of people and recognition that one life is as valuable as another?

Irvin L. Horowitz, *Genocide: State Power and Mass Murder*

Before Claude Neal died, he had experienced in full measure the dehumanization which accompanied violence. He had been denied the legal sanctuary of a jail, a trial by jury, solace from his friends in his last hours, his sexual identity, and finally his life. The basis of that dehumanization had begun, of course, much earlier. In a sense, he was only its victim. It began with the institution of slavery and assumption by colonists and later American whites that blacks were inferior. Debasing images of blacks typically served aspirations of planters and whites. The use of vigilante justice by whites against blacks was consistent with the frontier spirit which animated the planters' attitudes throughout the antebellum South. When the secure rewards of white supremacy were threatened by abolitionists and the Civil War, and then undermined during Reconstruction, whites fought back after 1877 and quickly reestablished their supremacy.

The new social order, which was firmly established by 1900, assured continuous gains by whites from blacks, especially those of obtaining a menial work force, enjoying feelings of social superiority, and using black women sexually. These gains explained the insistence of southerners on conformist attitudes toward race among their fellow whites. This process resulted in near extinction of free thought on matters which even remotely affected race relations and, in Cash's words, in a "crushing of dissent as it has not been established in any Western people since the decay of medieval feudalism."[1]

Impressive findings have related conformist pressures in child-rearing and social organization to violent attitudes and vigilante action against marginal groups. A person raised in this type of society is shown little tolerance, and when he grows up he extends little to others. But since he has developed small confidence in his own value because of constant pressures to do what is socially acceptable, he cannot become psychologically independent. His anger over his raising is easily displaced on weak people who cannot fight back, in this case the inferior social caste. He is readily disposed to calling another person "nigger" and, after having done that might next, if he feels he can get away with it, consider lynching that person. Violence of this type might also result, as Fromm suggested, from joylessness as well as cowardice since exploitatory societies breed lifelessness. Lynchings from this perspective provided a skeletal feast, at times almost enough life to be a carnival.

The negative images of blacks were fixed points in the social and intellectual compass of whites in the South of 1900. Stereotypes of their being ignorant, shiftless, and thieving were surely damaging enough to keep them under continuous suspicion, but allegations that they had abnormal cravings for white women served as a virtual call to arms. Whites used rape as an alarm signal to preserve their own solidarity as well as to attack uppity blacks, but their frequent lynching of blacks accused of rape established that they had real fears for the safety of their women as well. Indeed, in some instances, "insolent blacks" may have been lynched for rape simply because whites believed that they were aggressive enough to seek white women. The small number of actual rapes of white women by black men, however (if blacks lynched for rape is an index), suggests that white males were genuinely bedeviled by anxieties of caste and sex.

The startling increase in lynchings of blacks in the South in the period 1880 to 1900 is partly explainable as terror to secure

1. W. J. Cash, *The Mind of the South* (New York: Knopf, 1941), 134.

effective power for whites which had been briefly undermined by Reconstruction. After 1900, lynchings became less prevalent as the South became more urban and modern. There was, however, widespread persistence of the practice into the 1930s despite the fact that white dominance was clear-cut and mob rule was an affront to national ideals and human progress. The sociological school of the 1930s, as well as later historians and sociologists whom they have influenced, generally assumed that southern whites employed lynching whenever they sensed their power was slipping. Like a whiff of grapeshot in Napoleonic times, a good lynching cleared the air and comforted white people with the feeling they were still in command. Evidence does demonstrate that fear for the preservation of an advantageous social order inspired revenge motives in some lynch mobs. This viewpoint can now be enriched, however, by recent findings in empirical and social psychology, and historical perspectives which come from the rapid decline and demise of lynching after the 1930s. This information suggests that whites did not employ mob violence against blacks simply because they found them threatening. Fearlessness also triggered vigilantism against blacks. Whites were conscious of their unlimited power over blacks and were willing to administer it through lynchings because they knew they could do so with impunity. In effect, they were realistically aware of what they could get away with.

In this context, the lynching of blacks in the modern South parallels other phenomena of human destructiveness such as genocide, rape, and child abuse and suggests a theory on the relationship of human aggression to personal liberty. Although Stanley Elkins saw fit to establish a strained analogy between slavery and concentration camps in Germany under the Nazis, it would probably be more fruitful to make comparisons between the specific practice of lynchings of blacks in the modern South and the fate of Jews in Germany in the 1930s.[2] The lynchers in Jackson

2. Stanley Elkins, *Slavery: A Problem in American Institutional and Intellectual Life* (Chicago: University of Chicago Press, 1959). For excellent commentary on Elkins, see John W. Blassingame, *The Slave Community: Plantation Life in the Ante-bellum South* (New York: Oxford University Press, 1979), 227–36.

County were probably not any more fearful for the consequences of their actions than the executioners at Auschwitz. Similarly, it was difficult to adhere to moral scruples to oppose violence either in Nazi Germany with its charismatic leader, who proclaimed "truths" about Jews, or in the South where dehumanizing attitudes were sanctioned by historical tradition. Adolph Eichmann, who administered the massive program for committing millions of Jews to "killing camps," professed that he heard no voices from the outside to arouse his conscience and that he was never reproached for the performance of his duties.[3] Similarly, the lynchers in Jackson County did not encounter serious opposition before or after the lynching of Neal. Both groups may have been bored as well. Eichmann experienced boredom in his civilian life before he became a party member, in contrast with his enormous elation in fulfilling the will of the Nazis.[4] Similar zeal is suggested in the long and distant hunt for Neal by various lynch parties. On one occasion Eichmann declared that he would have had a bad conscience if he bad not performed well his job of dispatching Jews to the death camps. It seems reasonable to assume that the lynch mob felt the same way, at least, about transporting Neal.

The response of Jews in Germany and blacks in Jackson County also showed corresponding traits. Both chose to accept aggression without retaliation when it was escalated against them. The Jews, as Raul Hilberg's standard work on the subject illustrates, were virtually helpless, and their responses were "characterized by almost complete lack of resistance."[5] Although there were instances of revolts in the concentration camps, the general picture is one of compliance with the Nazi program of murder. Jewish prisoners even did the work in the camps, probably in hope that they would be spared if they followed orders.[6]

3. Hannah Arendt, *Eichmann in Jerusalem: A Report on the Banality of Evil* (New York: Viking, 1948), 126, 131.
    4. *Ibid.*, 33, 105.
    5. Raul Hilberg, *The Destruction of European Jews* (Chicago: Quadrangle Press, 1961), 624–25, 639, 662–63.
    6. *Ibid.*, 624, 628. See also Robert J. Lifton, *History and Human Survival: Es-*

They dug their own graves. Among blacks in the South there was also a notable absence of self-defense or counteraggression over lynching. It was exceptional for a black editor to write that blacks should put towns to the torch after a lynching occurred and just as exceptional for them to do so.[7] Black leaders in Jackson County pleaded with whites not to seek vengeance on good blacks like themselves; blacks generally withdrew during the turbulent events of October, 1934, in Jackson County and then attempted to show no outward resentment over what happened. And, similar to many inmates of the death camps, Claude Neal was polite even as he was being destroyed, probably because he, like the Jews, could only think of doing what he was supposed to do in the crisis, as if magically this somehow would save him.

Susan Brownmiller has detected a similar pattern of provoking circumstances in rape. In fact she asserts that "rape is to women as lynching was to blacks."[8] For her, rape is inherent in a social stiuation in which males are raised to be confident of their aggression, hence potential rapists, while women are trained to be fearful of aggression, hence subject to intimidation and to rape. Brownmiller declares, "Force, or the threat of force, is the method used against her. . . . She is unfit for the contest. Femininity has trained her to lose."[9] Relying on research among rape victims, she noted that they were generally unwilling to fight and hence victimized by their own submissive behavior. Like the Jews in Nazi Germany or blacks in the South, women generally assumed they were powerless to resist because they had no outside strength on which to rely. They accepted man's superior physical strength, his cultural biases to exploit women sexually, and his domination of government and law enforcement as accomplished facts, thereby accommodating to the practices which

---

says on the Young and Old, Survivors and the Dead, Peace and War and on Contemporary Psychohistory (New York: Random House, 1970), 198–207.

7. David M. Tucker, "Miss Ida B. Wells and the Memphis Lynching," *Phylon,* XXXII(1971), 112–22.

8. Susan Brownmiller, *Against Our Will: Men, Women, and Rape* (New York: Simon and Schuster, 1975), 254.

9. *Ibid.,* 360.

"killed" their sisters. The rapist, on the other hand, was emboldened because he knew that his chances of being convicted were slim. Rapists, too, obtained rewards and suffered little punishment.

Susan Brownmiller's proposals for a solution to the problems closely resemble a formula which released blacks from the yoke of lynching. She hoped to expose the injustices of the social system which encouraged rape and to embarrass males, such as the police, for their complicity. She also wished to set up efficient governmental mechanisms to bring rape offenders quickly to trial and to apply stiff penalties upon conviction.[10] And she promoted the idea that women should learn better to defend themselves so that they could retaliate on the spot. She discovered in her karate training that "as we learned to place our kicks and jabs with precision we were actually able to inspire fear in the men."[11] Thus by exposure of the corrupt system, the application of more certain punishment to offenders, and women's self-defense, penalties would replace rewards and justice replace injustice.

An author of a major book on child abuse has entitled one of her chapters, "Children are Niggers."[12] What she meant to convey is that children, like blacks historically, are vulnerable to discriminatory treatment and arbitrary punishment. Violence towards children by their parents illustrates the typical situational threat to the dignity and relative freedom of persons by the socially powerful. The circumstances which contribute to the problems of abused children bear a remarkable resemblance to those which accompanied the lynching of Claude Neal. For child abusers as for lynchers, instigations outweigh inhibitions, and rewards in discharging aggressions are more tangible than the remote possibility of punishments.

In one study it was found that most child abusers had themselves been victims of abuse as children and like members of the

10. *Ibid.*, 389.
11. *Ibid.*, 403.
12. Naomi F. Chase, *A Child is Being Beaten: Violence Against Children, an American Tragedy* (New York: Holt, Rinehart and Winston, 1975), 25–45.

lynch mob could condone their actions based on precedent.[13] Like the lynch mob which was accustomed to thinking of blacks in impersonal terms, those who victimized children were deficient in their "mothering sense" and therefore insensitive to the real needs of their children. They also were, like abusers of blacks, known to see dependents as scapegoats and to displace aggressions on them. Since children are relatively helpless, this could be done with impunity. It is interesting to note, however, that children who received the greatest abuse were those who were old enough to express some individuality and, at the same time, least able to protect themselves. David Gil observed that the ages of greatest abuse toward children were from three to nine. From age nine to age fifteen the incidence decreased to about the same number as when the child was one or two. The infant needed little discipline because he or she was too dependent and did not invite abuse; the older child could avoid it by ruses and skillful escapes; like blacks in the South in the period 1880–1935, who were neither slaves nor able to get away, children from three to nine were vulnerable because they could not defend their modest independence. And effective punishment for the victimizers like the lynchers was virtually nonexistent because even when cases were reported, which was unlikely because child-abusing parents tended to be socially isolated, criminal charges were seldom brought against parents.[14]

The common denominators between conditions which resulted in the lynching of American blacks and these other practices which produced human abuse lead to a hypothesis with broad implications: men become violent when they feel justified to do so and when they do not meet effective opposition to their pretensions.

Negative stereotypes of blacks were sufficient to justify lynchings. The assurances of a charismatic leader provided a rationale for the bloodbath against the Jews, and cultural norms in Ameri-

---

13. David G. Gil, *Violence Against Children* (Cambridge, Mass.: Harvard University Press, 1970), 32–33.
    14. *Ibid.*, 105, 125.

can society have apparently justified both rape and child abuse. Dehumanization of the victim was implicit in each justification for attacks against "niggers," impure Jews, "dumb broads," and "damned kids." The group minimized can be readily seen as over-stepping its boundaries since definitions of what is appropriate for it have been rigidly determined by those in control. At this point the critical question becomes whether the will to power feeds on the will to submit. Violence which implements that power apparently abhors a vacuum. Its executors may suffer from a sense of personal impotence and thereby add a special quality of rage to their actions. Hitler was an astounding misfit and prob-ably was sexually impotent, the parents who abuse children are often very poor, and the rapist is unsatisfied by a reciprocal sexual relationship. The lynch mob in Jackson County also felt "second-class" and the poor whites who comprised most lynch parties felt even less important. The critical issue in all of their actions, however, is not their peculiar personality disorders, but the fact that they are in positions to unleash violence with little if any fear of being hurt in return. Information to establish that victim-izers begin to relinquish their abuses, once they are exposed and vulnerable to counterattack, is probably best substantiated in connection with the lynching of blacks. However, the successful allied offensive in World War II forced a reassessment by German leaders of their policies toward Jews and supporters of women's rights are at least as confident that laws and a few karate lessons will do the same for them.

Successful retaliation can assume many forms. It is essential only that victims or their friends be aware of their plight and that they act to correct it. This can be done by example (self-defense), exposure of injustice through education (consciousness-raising), and the use of government. The democratic slogan that vigilance is the price of freedom assumes a new and convincing meaning if one adds that the will to defend that freedom is probably more important than the vigilance itself.

The importance of these insights from several examples of power-dependence relationships is relevant to the role of minority groups in a democracy. The problem of the lynching of blacks presents a classic model to establish these implications.

How are poor people, different people, and weak people to enjoy freedom in the face of the establishment's pressures and the righteousness of the majority?

In America there is hope, again with the experience of lynching in mind, that an ethic has distilled from successful national experience which can facilitate the inclusion of vulnerable groups. If these groups are able to organize their defense, many others, because of this ethic, will eventually join them and help reduce their burdens. In effect, the American social system is sustained by an abiding national conscience as the record on lynching affirms. Even before push comes to shove, it provides a basis for healthy self-correction.

Although numerous theories purportedly explain the lynching of blacks in the twentieth-century South, none of them are entirely satisfactory, singly or collectively. People have been frustrated and lived in poor environments without resorting to similar violence. The frontier in the South was not nearly so violent on whites as blacks, and we recently have witnessed the dissolution of the caste system in the modern South, including its most severe taboos against interracial sex, without a revival of lynchings. The theory that lynching served as a critical outlet for sexual tensions also seems less cogent as blacks and whites live together more freely yet without recourse to mob action and summary justice.

Lynchers, as the Claude Neal case attests, primarily responded with unlimited aggression because they were unbridled in the exercise of their power. Paradoxically, these excesses facilitated their demise. The lynchers gradually lost control over their microcosm as urbanization and education progressed in the twentieth century with a consequent decline in black lynch victims. This progress was dramatically illustrated and to some extent facilitated by the lynching of Claude Neal on October 27, 1934.

Selected
Bibliography

BOOKS, PAMPHLETS, AND REPORTS

Adorno, T. W., *et al. The Authoritarian Personality.* New York: Harper, 1950.

Agee, James, and Walker Evans. *Let Us Now Praise Famous Men.* Boston: Houghton Mifflin, 1941.

Arendt, Hannah. *Eichmann in Jerusalem: A Report on the Banality of Evil.* New York: Viking, 1948.

Berkowitz, Leonard. *Aggression: A Social Psychological Analysis.* New York: McGraw-Hill, 1962.

Brown, Richard M. *Strain of Violence: Historical Studies of American Violence and Vigilantism.* New York: Oxford University Press, 1975.

Brownmiller, Susan. *Against Our Will: Men, Women, and Rape.* New York: Simon and Schuster, 1975.

Carr, Robert K. *Federal Protection for Civil Rights: Quest for a Sword.* Ithaca: Cornell University Press, 1947.

Carter, Dan T. *Scottsboro: A Tragedy of the American South.* Baton Rouge: Louisiana State University Press, 1969.

Carver, Charles. *Brann and the Iconoclast.* Austin: University of Texas Press, 1957.

Cash, W. J. *The Mind of the South.* New York: Knopf, 1941.

Chadbourn, James Harmon. *Lynching and the Law.* Chapel Hill: University of North Carolina Press, 1933.

Chafe, William H. *The American Woman.* New York: Oxford University Press, 1972.

Chase, Naomi F. *A Child is Being Beaten: Violence Against Children, an American Tragedy.* New York: Holt, Rinehart and Winston, 1975.

Commission on Interracial Cooperation. *The Mob Still Rides: A Review of the Lynching Record, 1931–1935.* Atlanta: Commission on Interracial Cooperation, n.d.

Cutler, James E. *Lynch Law: An Investigation into the History of Lynching in the United States.* New York: Longmans, Green, 1905.

Davis, Allison, Burleigh B. Gardner, and Mary R. Gardner. *Deep South: A Social Anthropological Study of Caste and Class.* Chicago: University of Chicago Press, 1941.

Day, Beth. *Sexual Life Between Blacks and Whites: The Roots of Racism.* New York: World, 1972.

Dollard, John. *Caste and Class in a Southern Town.* Garden City, N.Y.: Doubleday, 1957.

Dykeman, Wilma, and James Stokely. *Seeds of Southern Change: The Life of Will Alexander.* Chicago: University of Chicago Press, 1962.

Elkins, Stanley. *Slavery: A Problem in American Institutional and Intellectual Life.* Chicago: University of Chicago Press, 1959.

Frederickson, George M. *The Black Image in the White Mind: The Debate on Afro-American Character and Destiny, 1871–1914.* New York: Harper and Row, 1971.

Fromm, Erich. *The Anatomy of Human Destructiveness.* New York: Holt, Rinehart and Winston, 1973.

Gaston, Paul. *The New South Creed: A Study in Southern Mythmaking.* New York: Knopf, 1970.

Genovese, Eugene. *Roll Jordan Roll: The World the Slaves Made.* New York: Pantheon, 1974.

Gil, David G. *Violence Against Children.* Cambridge, Mass.: Harvard University Press, 1970.

Ginzburg, Ralph. *100 Years of Lynching.* New York: Lancer Books, 1962.

Grant, Donald L. *The Anti-Lynching Movement, 1883–1932.* San Francisco: R and E Research Associates, 1975.

Grimshaw, Allen D., ed. *Racial Violence in the United States.* Chicago: Aldine, 1969.

Grubbs, Donald H. *Cry from the Cotton: The Southern Tenant Farmers' Union and the New Deal.* Chapel Hill: University of North Carolina Press, 1971.

Hall, Jacquelyn Dowd. *Revolt Against Chivalry: Jessie Daniel Ames and the Woman's Campaign Against Lynching.* New York: Columbia University Press, 1979.

Hilberg, Raul. *The Destruction of European Jews.* Chicago: Quadrangle Press, 1961.

Horowitz, Irving L. *Genocide: State Power and Mass Murder.* New Brunswick: Transaction Press, 1976.

Hurston, Zora N. *Mules and Men.* New York: Negro Universities Press, 1969.

Johnson, Charles S. *Growing Up in the Black Belt: Negro Youth in the*

Rural South. Washington: American Council on Education, 1941.

Johnson, James Weldon. *Autobiography of an Ex-Colored Man*. New York: Avon, 1965.

Jordan, Winthrop. *White over Black: American Attitudes Toward the Negro, 1550–1812*. Chapel Hill: University of North Carolina Press, 1968.

Justice, Blaine and Rita. *The Abusing Family*. New York: Human Sciences Press, 1976.

Kellogg, Charles. *NAACP: A History of the National Association for the Advancement of Colored People*. Baltimore: Johns Hopkins Press, 1967.

Kovel, Joel. *White Racism: A Psychohistory*. New York: Pantheon, 1970.

Mays, Benjamin F. *Born to Rebel: An Autobiography*. New York: Scribner's, 1971.

Moton, Robert R. *What the Negro Thinks*. Garden City, N.Y.: Doubleday, 1929.

Myrdal, Gunnar, Richard Sterner, and Arnold Rose. *An American Dilemma: The Negro Problem and Modern Democracy*. New York: Harper and Row, 1944.

National Association for the Advancement of Colored People. *The Lynching of Claude Neal*. New York: National Association for the Advancement of Colored People, 1934.

———. *Thirty Years of Lynching in the United States, 1889–1918*. New York: National Association for the Advancement of Colored People, 1919.

Newby, I. A. *Jim Crow's Defense: Anti-Negro Thought in America, 1900–1930*. Baton Rouge: Louisiana State University Press, 1965.

Nolan, Charles H. *The Negro's Image in the South*. Lexington: University of Kentucky Press, 1967.

Ransom, Roger L., and Richard Sutch. *One Kind of Freedom: The Economic Consequences of Emancipation*. Cambridge: Cambridge University Press, 1977.

Raper, Arthur F. *The Tragedy of Lynching*. Chapel Hill: University of North Carolina Press, 1933.

Rhyne, Janie Smith. *Our Yesterdays*. Marianna: n.p., 1968.

Rosenbaum, H. Jon, and Peter C. Sederberg, eds. *Vigilante Politics*. Philadelphia: University of Pennsylvania Press, 1976.

Rosengarten, Theodore. *All God's Dangers: The Life of Nate Shaw*. New York: Avon, 1974.

Scammon, Richard M., ed. *America at the Polls: A Handbook of American Presidential Election Statistics, 1920–1964*. Pittsburgh: University of Pittsburgh Press, 1965.

Scott, Anne Firor. *The Southern Lady: From Pedestal to Politics, 1830–1930*. Chicago: University of Chicago Press, 1970.

Shofner, Jerrell H. *Nor Is It Over Yet: Florida in the Era of Reconstruction, 1863–1877*. Gainesville: University of Florida Press, 1974.

Spear, Allan H. *Black Chicago: The Making of a Negro Ghetto: 1840–1930*. Chicago: University of Chicago Press, 1967.

Swisher, Carl B., ed. *Selected Papers of Homer Cummings, Attorney General of the United States, 1933–1939*. New York: Scribner's, 1939.

Tindall, George B. *South Carolina Negroes, 1877–1900*. Baton Rouge: Louisiana State University Press, 1952.

Vance, Rupert B. *Human Factors in Cotton Culture: A Study in the Social Geography of the American South*. Chapel Hill: University of North Carolina Press, 1929.

Van den Berghe, Pierre L. *Race and Racism: A Comparative Perspective*. New York: Wiley, 1967.

Waskow, Arthur I. *From Race Riot to Sit-In, 1919 to the 1960s*. Garden City, N.Y.: Anchor, 1966.

White, Walter. *A Man Called White: The Autobiography of Walter White*. New York: Viking, 1948.

————. *Rope and Faggot: A Biography of Judge Lynch*. New York: Knopf, 1929.

Williams, Daniel T., comp. *Eight Negro Bibliographies*. New York: Kraus Reprint Co., 1970.

Witherspoon, M. E. *Somebody Speak for Katy*. New York: Dodd and Mead, 1950.

Wolters, Raymond. *Negroes and the Great Depression: The Problem of Economic Recovery*. Westport, Conn.: Greenwood Press, 1970.

Wright, Richard. *Black Boy: A Record of Childhood and Youth*. Reprint. New York: Harper and Row, 1966.

ARTICLES

Bandura, Albert. "Influence of Models' Reinforcement Contingencies on the Acquisition of Imitative Responses." *Journal of Personality and Social Psychology*, I (1965), 589–95.

Cox, Merlin G. "David Sholtz: New Deal Governor of Florida." *Florida Historical Quarterly*, XLIII (1964), 142–52.

Dabney, Virginius. "Dixie Rejects Lynching." *Nation*, CVL (November 27, 1937), 579–81.

Donnerstein, M. and E. "Variables in Interracial Aggression: Potential Ingroup Censure." *Journal of Personality and Social Psychology*, XXVII (1975), 143–50.

————, et al.. "Variables in Interracial Aggression: Anonymity, Expected Retaliation, and a Riot." *Journal of Personality and Social Psychology*, XXII (1972), 236–45.

Grimshaw, Allen D. "Lawlessness and Violence in America and Their Special Manifestations in Changing White Relationships." *Journal of Negro History*, XLIV (January, 1959), 52–72.

Hackney, Sheldon. "Southern Violence." *American Historical Review*, LIIIV (February, 1969), 906–25.

Holmes, William F. "Whitecapping: Agrarian Violence in Mississippi, 1902–1906." *Journal of Southern History*, XXXV (May, 1969), 165–85.

Hovland, Carl, and R. Sears. "Correlations of Economic Indices with Lynchings." *Journal of Psychology*, IX (May, 1940), 301–10.

Miller, Robert M. "The Attitudes of American Protestantism Toward the Negro, 1919–1939." *Journal of Negro History*, XLI (July, 1956), 215–40.

Mintz, Alexander, "Re-examination of Correlation Between Lynchings and Economic Indices." *Journal of Abnormal and Social Psychology*, IV (1946), 154–65.

Schweinhaut, Henry A. "The Civil Liberties Section of the Department of Justice." *Bill of Rights Review*, I (1940–41), 205–12.

Zangrando, Robert L. "The NAACP and a Federal Antilynching Bill, 1934–1940." *Journal of Negro History*, L (April, 1965), 106–17.

GOVERNMENT DOCUMENTS

Federal Emergency Relief Administration. "Unemployment Relief Census." Florida File, National Archives, Washington.

Florida State Board of Health. *Annual Report, 1936.* Jacksonville: Florida State Board of Health, 1937.

Florida State Census, 1915. Tallahassee: n.p., 1915.

———, 1935. Winter Park, Florida: Orange Press, n.d.

———, 1925. N.p., n.d.

Jackson County Records. Jackson County Courthouse, Marianna, Florida.

Punishment for the Crime of Lynching: Hearings Before a Subcommittee of the Committee on the Judiciary, United States Senate. 73d Cong., 2d Sess., on S. 1978, February 20–21, 1934.

Punishment for the Crime of Lynching: Hearing Before a Subcommittee of the Committee on the Judiciary, United States Senate. 74th Cong., 1st Sess., on S. 24, February 14, 1935.

Report of the Adjutant General of the State of Florida: 1933, 1934. Tallahassee: n.p., 1934.

To Prevent and Punish the Crime of Lynching: Hearings Before a Subcommittee of the Committee on the Judiciary, United States Senate. 69th Cong., 1st Sess., on S. 121, February 16, 1926.

NEWSPAPERS

All newspapers were consulted for the period October 25 through November 10, 1934, unless otherwise specified.
Atlanta *Constitution*, 1934–1937.
Baltimore *Sun*.
Birmingham *News-Age-Herald*.
Boston *Herald*.
Brewton *Standard*.
Chicago *Daily Tribune*.
Chipley *Banner*.
DeFuniak Springs *Herald*.
Dothan *Eagle*.
Jackson County *Floridan* (Marianna *Floridan*), 1925–1935.
Marianna *Daily Times-Courier*, 1926–1935.
Montgomery *Advertiser*.
New York *Times*
Panama City *Pilot*.
Pensacola *Journal*.
Richmond *Times-Dispatch*.
Tallahassee *Democrat*.
Tampa *Tribune*.
Washington County *News*.
Washington *Post*.

MANUSCRIPT COLLECTIONS

Ames, Jessie Daniel. Papers. Southern Historical Collection, University of North Carolina, Chapel Hill.
Association of Southern Women for the Prevention of Lynching. Papers. Trevor-Arnett Library, Atlanta University, Atlanta, Georgia.
Bethune, Mary McLeod. Papers. Amistad Research Center, Dillard University, New Orleans, Louisiana.
Commission on Interracial Cooperation. Papers. Trevor-Arnett Library, Atlanta University, Atlanta, Georgia.
Cone, Governor Fred P. Papers. Florida State Archives, Tallahassee.
Kester, Howard A. Papers. Southern Historical Collection, University of North Carolina, Chapel Hill.
Lynching Records. Tuskegee Institute Archives, Tuskegee, Alabama.
Miller, Governor B. M. Papers. Alabama State Archives, Montgomery.
National Association for the Advancement of Colored People. Papers. Manuscript Division, Library of Congress.
Roosevelt, Eleanor. Papers. Franklin D. Roosevelt Library, Hyde Park, New York.

Roosevelt, Franklin Delano. Papers. Franklin D. Roosevelt Library, Hyde Park, New York.
Sholtz, Governor David. Papers. Florida State Archives, Tallahassee.

THESES AND DISSERTATIONS

Burrows, Edward F. "The Commission on Interracial Cooperation." Ph.D. dissertation, University of Wisconsin, 1954.
Reeder, Jesse. "Federal Efforts to Control Lynching." M.A. thesis, Cornell University, 1952.
Zangrando, Robert L. "The Efforts of the National Association for the Advancement of Colored People to Secure Passage of a Federal Anti-Lynching Law." Ph.D. dissertation, University of Pennsylvania, 1963.

Index